BUILD A BUSINESS YOU LOVE

A man's heart plans his way,
*but the L*ORD *directs his steps.*
—Proverbs 16:9 NKJV

BUILD A BUSINESS YOU LOVE

Mastering the 5 Stages
of Business

DAVE RAMSEY

RAMSEY
P R E S S

CONTENTS

ACKNOWLEDGMENTS

The irony is not lost on me that this book has actually been produced because Ramsey Solutions is the product of the information on the pages. The team that birthed this project is amazing. I'd like to say a special thanks to . . .

John Felkins, who has been key at formulating these principles and personally making sure they were put down on these pages.

Michelle Grooms, whose care and talent made sure John's and my words conformed somewhat to the English language—all the while being a world-class storyteller.

Rick Prall, for your commitment to excellence and your outstanding research and editorial support.

ACKNOWLEDGMENTS

Preston Cannon, our longtime Executive Director of Ramsey Press, guiding the production and launch of yet another Ramsey book.

And thanks to all the small-business people that I have had the privilege of teaching and befriending over all these years through EntreLeadership. You are truly the heartbeat of the American economy, and we love you.

INTRODUCTION

I recently had the chance to play a couple of famous golf courses in Scotland. All you golf nuts will know the courses I'm talking about, and you'll understand what a once-in-a lifetime opportunity that is. The thing is, on both days, on both courses, we were dealing with fog so bad, we couldn't even see forty yards ahead of us. Certainly not ideal for an opportunity like that, but we'd paid a good bit of money to get on those courses, and we were not going to miss the chance!

We had great service and awesome caddies at both courses. At the first course, at each hole, our caddie would point at the fog bank in front of us in the general direction of the fairway and tell us, "Hit in that direction, then we'll walk down there and hopefully find your ball." Imagine tee-ing up and trying to hit a two-hundred-yard drive into noth-ingness. It's really, really difficult to swing a golf club as hard as you can when you have no freaking idea where the ball needs to go. Needless to say, it took a long time to play that course, and I wondered more than once how many cases of golf balls it's possible to lose in one round.

The next course we played was Kingsbarns, and we had the exact same conditions—thick fog and an excellent caddie to guide us. But there was one incredibly simple, incredibly effective difference: At Kingsbarns, the staff placed stakes with flashing red battery-operated lights every fifty yards or so to mark the direction of the fairway. That one detail changed everything. We were still hitting into the nothingness of the fog, but the lights allowed us to see far enough ahead to know we were hitting in the right direction. That little bit of hope gave us the confidence and energy to play better, faster and have more fun. All because of those little red lights marking the way.

In the nearly forty years I've been in business, I've felt like I was staring straight into a fog bank more times than I can count. All I could see was the crisis in front of me. My perspective went no further than the end of my nose. I was just trying to do the next right thing. And the next right thing after that. And I never thought about doing it a different way. But if someone had told me there was a system for growing my business—an actual path with little blinking red markers to guide me—that may not have eliminated all the false starts and mistakes I made, but it would have limited them. And I would have been able to see past the current crisis of the day and have hope and confidence that my business was on the right path.

That's my goal for business owners reading this book. Even though you're often working in foggy conditions, the principles you'll learn in this book will mark the path clearly enough to give you the hope and confidence you need to give it your all and keep your business moving forward. And on occasion, the sun will break through, and a breeze will blow the fog away, and you will know exactly what to do and when. You'll avoid the false starts and the mistakes. And as a result, you'll build *your* business faster, stronger, and better than I built my own.

Are you ready? Game on!

THE SIX DRIVERS OF BUSINESS

A journalist once asked me, "Did you ever dream your business would get this big?"

"Of course I did!" I shot back. Then I confessed, "I just never imagined how much work it would take to get here."

You already know this, but running your own business is hard—really hard. As nice as it would be to have an easy button for running a business, there just isn't one. To make matters worse, most people around you don't understand all you go through to get your business up and running—or to keep it on the rails. You've got to manage the cost of goods, production issues, and hiring and training team members, along with managing a customer base. You have to master your insecurities, overcome a mountain of mistakes, and conquer the chaos of all that comes with running a company.

There are a lot of theories in the marketplace about how to run a business. But you don't need theories—you need to hear from someone who's actually made this work. Someone who got a lot of bruises and scars along the way. Those scars remind me of the struggles—and I'm sure you have plenty of scars too.

If you're here wanting a tenured college professor to give you some proper scientific theory about leadership—someone who's never had to make payroll, by the way—you're in the wrong place. I've done all the stuff in this book. I've made all the mistakes. All of them! My team and I survived our mistakes, and every year we got a little bit better. This book will guide you through the steps you'll need to take to actually help your business grow. That's what you want—and it's the same thing that most small-business owners want—to see your business grow.

What you're going to find in this book is evidence of what works. Proven practices. You're going to find wisdom from the trenches. And you're going to hear from other business leaders like you who are trying to figure this out. Just understand this on the front end: We don't sell microwaves—we're in the crockpot business. This doesn't happen overnight.

Success in business comes from decades of scratching, clawing, grinding, getting up before dawn, getting a little better—then repeat: get up, get a little better, get up, get a little better. Why? Because we all suck when we start. I did—and you do too. That's not mean, it's just reality. So you've got to get a little better every day. And if you keep showing up, you *will* get better and you *will* win at business!

When I think back to the question that reporter asked, the truth is, if I'd known how hard running a business was going to be, I might not have done it. Really. It was brutal in those early days. It was a lot of hard work and long hours. You've been there—you might be there right now. Back then, I realized I was the biggest problem when it came to growing this business. Yes, me—the man in the mirror. I recognized that I didn't know a lot of stuff and I would need a new level of knowledge, a new level of experience, a new level of sophistication, and a new level of wisdom if I was going to get where I needed to go. I've learned how to get better, how to move things forward, and how to leverage my team for greater results.

One of the most effective ways I found to grow personally—to get a little better every day—was through reading. I've read a lot of books from some of the smartest people on the planet. And a lot of those people have become good friends now, including Dr. Henry Cloud, John Maxwell, Pat Lencioni, and Jim Collins. When I started reading their books, I just wanted to have one-tenth of one percent of their intellect to help me move this business a little further along. If you've read my first book on business and leadership, *EntreLeadership*, you know their wisdom has been incredibly impactful in how I run my business—and you'll certainly recognize some of their pieces of advice as you read through this book.

THE SOLUTION

I'm going to spend most of the pages in this book walking you through the Five Stages of Business: Treadmill Operator, Pathfinder, Trailblazer, Peak Performer, and Legacy Builder. The stages are mile markers, seasons, and levels of maturity. Call them what you want, but you're going to go through them in your business—and each one has its own special challenges.

But before I start talking about what defines those stages, there are six fundamental truths related to business growth and success that you need to understand. We discovered these principles through three decades of firsthand experience and insight gathered from tens of thousands of business owners. They're called the Six Drivers of Business—because that's what they do, they drive your business forward and are essential for its success:

Personal: You're both the problem and the solution.

Purpose: Business is about more than just the bottom line.

People: A unified team is key to winning.

Plan: Success is intentional; it doesn't happen by accident.

Product: Serve enough people and the revenue will follow.

Profit: Profits fuel your purpose.

As you've probably already figured out, you never truly arrive in business; you just continually refine and master these skills. That's why the six drivers are designed to build on one another in a continuous cycle you'll keep working for as long as you're in business.

These drivers are the foundation of what you do, how you lead, and how you propel your business through the five stages we'll cover in the rest of this book. Like a waterwheel, each driver leads to the next. As you fill up the bucket in one driver, what you learn starts to pour into the next. That forward momentum takes you and your business to where you need—and want—to go. But if you try to skip a driver, the whole thing will come to a screeching halt. If you try to skip two of them, it will freeze up. Just as a waterwheel doesn't work like that, neither does your business when it comes to these drivers—you've got to get it turning, and as you keep putting the water in, it keeps spinning.

Don't get confused though. The drivers aren't a checklist. One rotation through the drivers does not mean you automatically move to the next stage of business. Often, each stage of business will require multiple rotations through the drivers. In fact, we've learned there isn't a strict correlation between which stage of business you're in and how many times you'll go around the wheel of drivers.

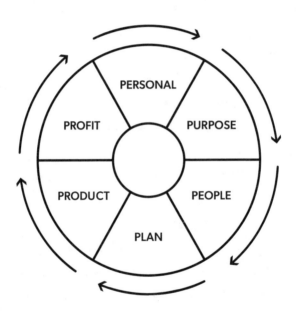

Business is a marathon. Not a sprint. Winning in business doesn't happen quickly, and it doesn't happen easily. It's a process, and it's frustrating a lot of the time.

I don't know about you, but when I'm learning something new, I get a little bit mad—mad because there's one more thing to learn and mad because I don't want to do this. It feels weird. It's uncomfortable. It's not the way I've always done business. But the way I did things in the past only got us to this point. If I'm going to continue to grow this business, I've got to do something different than what I've always done. The same is true for you. As I pointed out earlier, you must master the Six Drivers of Business to create the growth you need, both in your leadership and your business, to move through the Five Stages of Business. When you master the drivers, you gain the skills, competencies, and knowledge you need to level up to the next stage.

To make this system work, you're always making minimum payments on all the drivers all the time. That just means, no matter which stage of business you find yourself in, you'll always be working to improve in each of these drivers. You can't neglect any of them. You may focus a bit more on one or two in a season, but each stage will require you to do some work in each driver. And one last thing before we dig into the drivers: Remember that every business and every business owner is different. That means you'll work through the drivers and progress through the stages differently from other business owners.

All right. Let's see what the Six Drivers of Business are all about.

DRIVER 1: PERSONAL

You're Both the Problem and the Solution

The first driver of business is Personal—it all starts with the person in the mirror. That would be *you*. Organizations are never limited by their opportunity; they're limited by their leader. The reality, if you're willing to face it, is that you're the problem—and you're also the solution. That's why this first driver is related to personal development. My good friend and bestselling author John Maxwell talks about the Law of the Lid, which says how well you lead will determine how well you succeed. In other words, your ability to lead—or lack of ability to lead—is the lid to your business's growth.

The good news is that becoming a better leader is a choice. Leadership is a skill you can improve. No matter where you are as a leader today, you can make the decision to become a *better* leader. And you'll need to make that decision over and over. We have a saying at Ramsey: "If you're not growing, you're dying." What that means for you as a business owner is, if you're not growing to be the leader who can meet the challenges of each stage of business, there's no way for your business to move from one stage to another.

For well over a decade, I've asked groups of business leaders what words describe an excellent leader. I get a similar list each time I do this. It always includes words like *humble, servant, communicator, decisive, godly, integrity, visionary, passionate, loyal, influential,* and *driven.* Read over that list again. We're not in disagreement about the qualities that make a great leader. We just have trouble electing one. We just have trouble being one. We just have trouble hiring one, leading one, and growing people into that kind of leader.

To the extent that these words don't describe you, you're lacking as a leader. And here's the really interesting thing: Every one of those qualities of leadership is a decision. They're a choice you can make. They're personal character qualities you can work on. You don't have integrity? You can decide to become a person of fanatical integrity. You're not humble? You can choose to be humble. You're not decisive? Decision-making is a choice too.

In the first stage of business—Treadmill Operator—the Personal driver will require you to improve basic business skills, hard skills like time management, budgeting, hiring, and delegation. In the next stage, the Pathfinder, you'll broaden your view and work on the skills you need to lead a team, like how to cast vision, identify your core values, and create consistent communication. I'll unpack all that in the Pathfinder stage—and don't worry, it will all make sense as we walk through it together.

This driver—Personal—may be the hardest to master because it's all about you. It requires the most personal change so you can be the best possible leader. Maybe you have a lot of this handled already. Good! Maybe you read this and think, *Crap, I've got to change a lot about how I show up as a leader.* Either way, where you're headed is more important than where you've been. Time to get moving!

DRIVER 2: PURPOSE

Business Is About More than Just the Bottom Line

Your team needs to know why their work matters. It's important to hire people who are wired to show up every day and give their best, of course, but if your business is only about money, even those folks won't last long. Work that matters drives people to push through tough times. The Purpose driver is all about the purpose of your business or organization.

Don't skip this one. It's easy for hard-charging, business-minded people like us to just drive by this, thinking, *Oh, that's one of those cute little sayings on your brochure.* But your business's purpose goes a lot deeper than that and is a major focus of the Trailblazer stage. So expect to unpack some best practices around identifying and communicating your business's purpose when we get to that chapter.

Everybody—and every business—needs to know their why. That phrase, "your why," got a lot of attention when Simon Sinek published his book *Start with Why: How Great Leaders Inspire Everyone to Take Action.* Simon says the mission of your business begins with *why* or, more specifically, *why you are in business.* If your *why* isn't right, you'll quit when the money comes. Money is never enough—even if you can buy whatever you want. Trust me, I've eaten enough lobster to know it tastes like soap when you eat too much of it just because you can afford to.

Money's not the be-all and end-all, and it won't work as the primary goal for your business. Your team needs to know why their work matters. Why do you do what you do? At Ramsey Solutions, we say we exist for the people outside our walls. Our mission is to provide hope for everyone in every walk of life. That's a whole lot different than saying we work just to write books, create events, and put on a radio show. While we do all those things—and a lot more—*why* we do them is what drives us.

This is no different if you own, say, a car repair business. *Why* are you in the car repair business? Have you ever seen a single mom stranded on the side of the road with two little kids in the back of the car? At that moment, why you do your work matters to her. It's not just fixing a car—it's coming to the rescue of a family at a time of need. Or maybe you're a plumber. Just think about all the ways people's lives are disrupted when their hot water is out. Your services will keep a young family's kitchen running and their clothes and kids clean. Or maybe you do heat and air. In the winter, if someone's heat is out, that's an emergency. That's why your work matters.

I've met very few successful business owners whose only *why* was to make a boatload of money. If your business is just about money, you'll have problems with your team, and your customers will hate doing business with you. They can smell money-hungry people. Your *why* needs to reflect a higher calling and purpose. You're here to serve, and you're here to change people's lives—including the lives of your team members. That's when what you do actually matters. To help your team understand what's important to you and what drives your *why*, you need to clearly communicate your mission, your vision, and your values to them. These things need to be tattooed onto your soul and seared into the mind of your team.

One of our core values at Ramsey Solutions is Colossians 3:23 where the Apostle Paul wrote, "Whatever you do, work at it with all your heart, as working for the Lord" (NIV). That puts a different perspective on your work. I'm working with excellence because I'm working for the Lord, first and foremost.

Now, I'm not against making money. In fact, I want you to make a lot of money and win in business. But I also want your life to change, and I want your business to make a difference in people's lives along the way. A clearly defined purpose is necessary for both because it sets you up to spin around to the next driver on the wheel.

DRIVER 3: PEOPLE

A Unified Team Is Key to Winning

Business is easy until people get involved, right? That's the third driver of business: People. As someone who's been doing this for more than thirty years, I'll tell you that people are your biggest blessing—but they're also your biggest burden. To start with, in most businesses, payroll is the largest expense on the profit and loss statement (P&L). That makes people your biggest cost.

In business, every P&L item should generate a return on investment (ROI)—that includes payroll. That's right, you should expect a return on your investment from the people on your team. It took a while for me to realize how important this is. When I look at my P&L from an investment standpoint, it looks like I'm completely out of balance. With tens of millions of dollars in payroll every year, I'm way heavy on this one line item. So I need to see an ROI on that. That means, in order for Ramsey Solutions to be profitable, everybody on the team has to make more than they cost as a whole or we don't stay open. That's just basic economics.

Now, for a little while, I had "employees," and I never want another employee. And to this day, I don't. Employees come in late, leave early, and steal while they're there. Ramsey Solutions has over one thousand team members—and zero employees. But that didn't happen naturally or overnight. We spend a lot of focused time on our hiring process. It costs a lot of money to get a new team member hired, relocated, equipped, and trained. We learned the hard way that if we don't take our time to hire the right person, we'll end up spending way more money and time trying to replace that bad hire.

Once you have the right people on the team, you have to put in the work to keep that team unified. Zig Ziglar, an author and one of the great motivational speakers of his time, used the example of Belgian draft horses to explain the power of a unified team. Belgian draft horses are huge muscular animals, much like the Clydesdale horses you see on beer commercials. If you hook a Belgian draft horse to a sled, the typical horse, by itself, can pull eight thousand pounds. It's very impressive—that's the equivalent of two mid-size cars! If you put two unrelated Belgian draft horses together, they can pull twenty-four thousand pounds. That's a 3x increase instead of the 2x you expected.

Again, very impressive, but here's what's even more mind-blowing: If you combine a matched pair of Belgian draft horses, meaning they're siblings or cousins from the same farm that have been trained to work together, they can pull thirty-two thousand pounds—that's four times what a single horse can do! Now *that* is amazing!

So, what do horses have to do with building a unified team? When you put the very best people on your team—at Ramsey, we refer to them as thoroughbreds—and train them to be unified in pulling together to get the work done, amazing results happen. That's how a small team can have a huge impact for your business. It's not about the size of the team, it's about whether they've been trained together and work together. It's about the synergy and trust they develop with each other over time.

Of the Six Drivers of Business, People is the one where you'll likely spend the most time, experience the most heartache, but also get the most return. At Ramsey Solutions, we spend a ton of money on our team, putting on some incredible parties and team events each year. But we see plenty of ROI from those expenses through the team culture we've created, which, in turn, leads to super productive team members.

We spend a *lot* of time in other books, in our coaching, and in our events teaching how to build a team culture that is fun and productive, so we won't use up more space on that topic here. People and culture-building are a big focus in the Trailblazer stage, but you'll build on your People driver differently at each business stage. As you do, you'll eventually move to the next driver, which is Plan.

DRIVER 4: PLAN

Success Is Intentional; It Doesn't Happen by Accident

If you don't have a plan to move your business forward, guess what—it won't move forward or grow. Another one of my favorite statements from Zig Ziglar is, "If you aim at nothing, you will hit it every time." You can't move your company forward if you don't know where you're going. Obviously, the team can't move it forward if they don't know what forward is. You haven't told them—because you can't tell them something you haven't figured out.

The fourth driver of business is Plan. To win in business, you must develop a strategic mindset, not just a tactical one. This is definitely something you'll want to give attention to in every stage of business, and it becomes critically important when you get to the Peak Performer and Legacy Builder stages. I get it. As a business owner, you're all about the tactical—getting the work done. But listen, no NFL team ever wins the title by accident. They all nail down their plans before the season even starts. For every game a professional football team plays, they have a plan—their winning strategy. Most teams even script out their first ten plays so that everyone on the team knows exactly what to do to win. You can do a similar thing with your business.

I'll tell you, planning was one of my personal weak spots. As an entrepreneur, I'm very good at recognizing a need and filling it. I'm very tactical. I can look at a spreadsheet and say, "This is what's wrong. We've got to fix this." I can jump on a problem and get things done and get things moving. I'm going to push buttons, do what has to be done, and I'm going to push it through. That may not be your style, but it's who I am.

But I never did much planning. I just figured I could outsell and outwork my stupidity. I thought if we made enough revenue, it would make up for my lack of planning or any mistakes that I made. That might work for a while, but it also limits your growth. That mindset will keep you stuck in the early stages of business, and you won't be able to move forward.

Our plans at Ramsey Solutions today are much more sophisticated than the first ones we came up with. Today, our planning meetings are intentional and intense. We'll talk more about strategic planning in the Trailblazer stage, because that's when it becomes vital to your continued growth.

DRIVER 5: PRODUCT

Serve Enough People, and the Revenue Will Follow

The next driver of business is Product. The reality is that this is where most businesses start. They never bother with themselves, they never bother with purpose, and they never bother with the people. They just say, "Here's our product or here's our service. Now we need to go get some people to buy this." And about eight years later, they wonder why they're stuck. If that's the story of your business, that's okay. Just start where you are and work through the drivers. Then, when you've worked on Personal, Purpose, People, and Plan, you're ready to adjust your current product line so that it flows out of who you are, your purpose, your team's strengths, and your strategic plan.

In short, you're ready to deliver excellence. And if it feels like it took a long time to get here, that's because it did. In Proverbs 21:5, the Bible tells us the diligent prosper. Diligence is when you provide excellence every day and in everything you produce, consistently, over time. And to do that, you need excellent people doing excellent work that produces excellent results. When all that lines up, you can go into a proven industry that has its way of doing things and then completely disrupt that industry by bringing a level of excellence that never existed—until you came onto the scene.

Does excellence mean perfection? No. Sometimes you just have to get your product into the market even if it's not perfect. You have to choose progress over perfection. I've sold twenty million books with my name on them, and I've never sold a single book that didn't have at least one typo. Of course, our team edited the manuscript, and lots of people read through it. We tried our best, but it always seems that something slips through. If you wait until your product is perfect, you'll never get it to market. Entrepreneur and bestselling author Seth Godin, in his book *Linchpin*, says, "Ship it, ship it, ship it." Sure, you want things to be perfect, but perfection isn't the same thing as excellence. Business is a balancing act. Don't allow the pursuit of perfection to cause you to never ship it. A perfectionist can get paralysis of the analysis. Shoot for excellence in all you do and in all you offer, and get that excellent product to market so it can start making a difference for your customers and yield benefits for your business.

DRIVER 6: PROFIT

Profits Fuel Your Purpose

Profit is the natural result of business—when you do it correctly. That's why you'll pay attention to the Profit driver in every stage of business, but it's really important to get focused on what's producing profits—and how—in the first three stages.

When you bring a product or service to market that meets a need in someone's life, you make a profit, and you start making money. Now, you might have gotten lucky like I did and started making money before you knew these other things. So sure, you can make a certain level of money when you're flying by the seat of your pants. But we started making the level of money we're making now when I started working the Six Drivers of Business in order.

Never apologize for making a profit when you're doing it the right way. Making money with integrity is the point of capitalism—the free buying and selling of goods and services. You have the freedom to choose what you want to produce and sell, the freedom to choose the price you want to set or spend, and the freedom to choose what you want to buy and what services you want to use. Your customers also have those freedoms.

For years, we've had a bunch of people telling us that we should feel bad for making money, for busting our butts, and for putting goods and services into the marketplace. That's garbage! We didn't do anything wrong, and neither are you. You didn't steal from someone. You served someone, you helped someone, you changed someone's life in some way. If you hadn't made their life better, they wouldn't have given you any money. And if they keep coming back to buy from you again—and give you more money—they're saying, "Good job. Thank you."

Author and leadership/management consultant Ken Blanchard says profit is the applause you get from taking care of your customers. If your customers give you a lot of money, they're giving you a standing ovation! And my friend Rabbi Daniel Lapin wrote an incredible book called *Thou Shall Prosper* where he shares the idea that when you're good to your customers, they give you certificates of appreciation with presidents' faces on them. I love that!

We remind our team of this idea all the time: If you help enough people, you don't have to worry about money. We've helped millions of people with their money, their careers, their businesses, and their relationships. And God has chosen to bless our work in the form of financial success for the company.

For any business to be profitable, it must have a game plan called a budget, and that is a foundation you'll build in the Treadmill Operator stage. Without a budget, you'll never understand what's going on financially in your company. And business owners who don't stay on top of their numbers will fail. Period.

DRIVING BUSINESS

Personal, Purpose, People, Plan, Product, and Profit. Those are the Six Drivers of Business. At this point, Ramsey Solutions—the business I started in my living room over thirty years ago—has worked through these six drivers too many times to count. Each time, we've gotten a little better, and our business has grown and matured through the Five Stages of Business.

That's something I didn't understand thirty years ago—that business happens in stages. Now I know better, thanks to my own experience coupled with two decades of work with tens of thousands of small-business owners across the country who, like you, know how hard it is to turn a business idea into a growing business today. We didn't start out trying to write a book. We were just trying to solve our own problems while also helping other people solve theirs. We found specific, repeatable challenges every business has to face. And we found that those challenges define the different stages of business. Before we unpack those stages in detail in the chapters to come, let's take a quick look at each.

Treadmill Operator

The first stage of business is Treadmill Operator. That's where everyone starts. You might be there now, but you will remember it like it was yesterday—because it was. The Treadmill Operator just gets stuff done. They personally generate most of their business revenue, so they have no time for anything else. You're the CEO, the chief everything officer. You set up the chairs, you swing the hammer, you turn the wrench.

When I was at this stage, I was working my butt off every day, all day. But I felt like I was on a treadmill because I was putting in all this effort, but I wasn't getting anywhere. I'm sure you know the feeling—all you're doing is putting out fires, and if you stop running for a second, everything would grind to a screeching halt. You won't make payroll on

Friday, or you won't make rent. Whatever the work is, you've got to do it because you're the only one getting it done.

Pathfinder

The second stage of business is Pathfinder. At this stage, the key challenge you'll face is that your team lacks clear direction. By now, you've successfully delegated work to others so you're not having to do it all. You have a team helping generate revenue, but they may or may not be aligned to the purpose of the business. You've put some processes into place, and you've hired some new folks, but you're still spending a lot of time putting out fires. There's still a lot of chaos going on, and you find yourself bumping into stuff and course-correcting as you go. A healthy level of chaos is good in any business at any level, but at this stage, chaos is more of a mantra than it should be.

Trailblazer

The third stage is Trailblazer. Moving more clearly down the path, you now have some people on your team who get what your business is about. But you don't know how to scale what you've built. This is the stage where you realize you need additional layers of leadership to keep the business moving forward, so you begin by identifying team members who are leading naturally—not because you gave them a title. You'll also solidify your strategic plan and set longer-term goals for the business.

Peak Performer

The fourth stage is Peak Performer. This is a fun stage of business. You begin to feel the reward for your efforts, but you must guard your team and yourself from getting too comfortable. At this stage, your systems and processes are running well, and you feel like you're running a business rather than it running you. It's fun to watch your team take ownership and your leaders lead, but it will be up to you and your leadership team to adopt a culture of relentless improvement to keep your business from stalling out.

Legacy Builder

The fifth and final stage is Legacy Builder. At this stage, you're working through the steps to hand off the company to someone else—so your business can live on without you. Most small-business owners act as though they're immortal. They never consider what will happen to their business when they're gone. Dying simply is not part of the plan. I get it. Handing your business—your baby—over to someone else is extremely emotional. But without a succession plan, your business and all the work you put into it and all the good it can continue to do will end with you.

Drivers and Stages

At this point, you might be thinking, *Six drivers and five stages? What should I focus on? What's the relationship between the drivers and stages?* Here's what it boils down to: **As you work on the six drivers, your business will level up through the five stages.**

That's how this works. This is the EntreLeadership System—the method we used to grow from a card table in my living room to where we are today. Don't skim over this. If you grasp this core principle, it will unlock the rest of the book: Get better at the drivers and go further with your business in the stages. Remember, each of the six drivers leads to the next. That said, there are certain drivers you'll spend more time on depending on which stage your business is currently in. For example, a lack of team alignment won't hinder you if you don't have a team! But once you have a team, getting and keeping them all aligned is a major challenge.

These drivers work because they're cyclical. When you're constantly working on the drivers, you're constantly improving yourself and your business. Each time you come back to one of the drivers, you should be better at it than the last time you came around.

In the next chapters, we'll explore each of the Five Stages of Business. Occasionally, we'll identify specific drivers to focus on in each stage, but you'll devote a portion of your time to refining every driver in every stage. To help you visualize that, we'll give you access to a quick map of the stages—and the challenges specific to each stage—at the end of the chapter.

Now, before you take off and start doing stuff just based on the information I've shared up to this point, take the time to read about each of the Five Stages of Business. I'll spend more time unpacking all of this—plus you'll get to learn from my screw-ups. I'll also give you some specific things to consider and work on in each stage so you can level up! Again, there's no easy button for business, but it's a lot faster to follow a trail than create one. It may have taken me thirty years to build Ramsey Solutions, but I believe you can build your business faster than that.

Your Challenge

To get the most out of this book, here are four things to do:

1. Scan the QR code at the end of this chapter and take the survey to identify your stage of business.
2. Read the chapters on the stages.
3. Download the resources.
4. Work the system.

Make sure you read about each stage regardless of your current stage in business and even if you believe you're in one of the later stages. It can be a big reality check on your progress to read about the struggles and challenges in each stage. You might discover there's something you missed and can add to your operations.

The actions described in each stage are not checkboxes. You don't get a gold star and get to level up because you did something once. These actions are your inputs into your business. The outcome is that, as time moves on and you maintain intensity, you'll start to observe your business maturing.

Each stage builds upon the previous ones, and the skills required in the early stages—such as time management, delegation, budgeting, and hiring—are still important in the later stages. For instance, even if you're a Treadmill Operator focusing on these areas, you'll find that these foundational skills are necessary for winning in every stage. Be aware that you don't "own" a stage once your business has grown to that level. You *can* go backward! Essentially, you rent your stage—and the rent is due every day!

Scan the QR code below to get access to the Entre-Leadership System map and take the survey to identify your stage of business.

1

TREADMILL OPERATOR

KEY CHALLENGE:

Too much of your business relies on you.

WHAT WINNING LOOKS LIKE:

The majority of your business results are
now generated without you.

TREADMILL OPERATOR

I dropped onto the couch, exhausted. It was nearly midnight, and I'd just gotten home from teaching one of the eight *Financial Peace University* classes scheduled for that week.

"You look tired," my wife, Sharon, said. That was kind of her. For months, she'd basically been a single mom, running the household and raising our three kids while I worked sixteen-hour days. If anyone had the right to be tired, it was Sharon.

"I feel like a truck ran over me," I told her.

"What did you do today?" she asked.

What did I do today? I asked myself. Every day for the last few years had honestly been a blur. Ever since I started my financial counseling business, I'd had more clients to help and more work to do than I had hours in the day. As much as I wanted to, there was no time to think about how to scale the work I was doing. Even when I took the leap to bring on my first team members, the business was growing so fast that we all ended up working our tails off day after day.

But now, even though it seemed impossible that we could be even busier, things had kicked into a whole new gear. We figured we could help more people by teaching a finance class than we could through individual counseling. So we developed a curriculum and started teaching it in a small ballroom at the Holiday Inn across the street from our office. About 350 people packed into that ballroom to hear me, thirty-four-year-old Dave in a bad suit and armed with an overhead projector, teach how to take control of their money. We started with one class a week on Tuesday nights. It quickly grew to two nights, then three. Before we knew it, we were teaching classes every night of the week and twice on Saturdays.

So, when Sharon asked me what I'd done that day, it was easy to recall the routine I'd been following for what felt like years at that point. I'd gotten up before dawn to spend some time with my Bible and grab a cup of coffee before I headed to the office at 7:30. I'd spent the morning there, walking around like a human fire extinguisher, putting out this fire and that fire until it was time to do the radio show. Then, after three hours of hosting the show, I hustled over to the hotel to set up tables and chairs for that night's class.

The worst part of this process was setting up the old-school projector screen. That thing had like fifty snaps that held the screen onto the frame, and I had to snap every one of them. Once that was done, I rushed back to the office to shower and shave for the second time that day, then back to the hotel to teach the hour-long class. After class, we broke up into small groups. We flipped the beds up against the walls and pushed the furniture out of the way in all the sleeping rooms on the first floor of the hotel to turn them into discussion rooms. Once class was done, we put all those rooms back together, took down the tables, stacked the chairs, and unsnapped and folded up that stupid projector screen. That night, as most nights, I'd stayed late to pray with and coach a scared couple who needed reassurance that, yes, they would be able to dig out from under the mountain of debt that was crushing them.

Don't misunderstand—I've always loved my work. My passion then and now is providing people hope and showing them how to clean up their financial messes. But that season in my business had me stuck on a treadmill of never-ending physically and emotionally exhausting work. I knew I couldn't keep up that pace forever, but I also didn't know how or when this season would end. I still had the same problem I had when I started the business: I was producing the revenue and producing the product. I had too much work and too little time to think about what was next. I'd become the bottleneck for my business. I was a Treadmill Operator.

Most Treadmill Operators are like I was in those early days. You don't really own a business; you own a job. You own a job because if you don't work, you don't get paid. If you own a painting company and you do all the painting, guess what? You own a job. If you don't go to work, no painting happens, and that means nobody's getting paid, right? When you own a job and you're sick or get hurt, you're unemployed. Whatever the work is, you've got to do it because you're the only one getting it done. Being a Treadmill Operator might be the hardest stage of business because it all depends on you, and that includes the stuff you're good at and the stuff you're not good at or know nothing about. It can be a real struggle, and a lot of business owners get stuck in this stage.

The Treadmill Operator spends their time just getting day-to-day stuff done. They generate so much of their business revenue that they don't have time to do much else. They're too busy setting up the chairs, swinging the hammer, or turning the wrench to figure out what the next step for their business should be. When I was at this stage, I was working my butt off, but I felt like a rat in a wheel—just going in circles. You know the feeling. You can't stop for a second because if you do, you won't make this week's payroll or this month's rent. If any of this hits home for you, you're probably on the treadmill just like I was.

SIGNS YOU MAY BE IN THE
TREADMILL OPERATOR STAGE

You're working *in* your business way more than you're working *on* your business.

You can't take time off because no business would get done.

You can't take time off because you'd make no money.

You're at risk for burnout—physically and emotionally.

FRUSTRATIONS YOU FACE IN THE TREADMILL OPERATOR STAGE

You don't have enough time to grow your business.

You feel trapped by your business.

Business stops when you stop.

You can't take a vacation—and you don't remember what a vacation feels like.

Running a small business can be lonely, isolating work. Our Small-Business Labor Crisis Report 2023 shows nearly 14 million small-business owners (42 percent) feel alone when they're dealing with business problems and decisions. A whopping 18.6 million (56 percent) say they've dealt with burnout in the last year. Small-business owners get to the end of the day feeling emotionally and physically exhausted, even losing sleep because of their businesses. I don't say all that to discourage you. I'm pointing it out because while I know you *feel* alone, you're *not* alone. The Treadmill Operator stage is hard for everyone. Business owners who are in the Treadmill Operator stage say things like:

"I lost a key team member from an injury, and now I'm back to working in the business instead of on it. My phone won't stop blowing up. I know I need to hire someone, but I don't know where in the world I can get the time to train them. I'm working crazy hours, and I feel incredibly behind."

"If I don't have thirty to forty calls every day and fires to put out, then what do I do? I'd love to travel with my family, and I'd love to be able to go on a trip without my phone. But that would be one of the scariest days I can imagine."

"I'm stuck doing office work most of the time."

Sound familiar? Here's the irony of the Treadmill Operator stage: By successfully starting your own business, you built a trap—a trap made from success. By the very act of succeeding, you created a situation where you'll have more work than you can do by yourself. So, on one hand, congratulations! You beat the odds. Way to go, rock star! You know better than most that the calluses on your hands and your character, earned through stress and strain, are the trophies of service to others. You've accomplished way more than most people ever will, so hold your head high. But now the question becomes *How do I get out of this trap, and how do I get off the wheel?*

Getting off the Treadmill

The solution to getting off the treadmill is to get to a place where the majority of your business revenue can be generated without your being in the room. You do this by being diligent about how you use your time, about the people you hire, about the tasks you delegate, and about your numbers so you know you can afford the help. I started to get off the treadmill when I began delegating some of the coaching I was doing to my first team member, Russ Carroll. He was a semi-retired financial coach who joined forces with me in the early days of the business, working on straight commission because I couldn't afford to pay him a salary at the time. Once I wasn't the only one handling clients, I could spend time on planning and goal setting that would grow the business while he was generating revenue.

The second big step we took was putting *Financial Peace University* (FPU) on video tape (yep, good ol' VHS!). To be honest, I didn't think it would work. I even snuck into one of the first classes using the taped version of FPU and stood in the back of the room while the class watched the video. As I was teaching on the tape, I told people to raise their hands. The audience on tape raised their hands—and so did the people in the live FPU class! When I told a joke, the entire class laughed! It blew my mind, and believe me, I was happy to be wrong because then I knew we were onto something. With the class on video, we could sell these tapes and people everywhere could take FPU. It was another way the business could make money when I wasn't in the room. It was a game changer! People, products, or processes that generate revenue without you are essential for growing your business past the Treadmill Operator stage. I can't tell you what those key people, products, and processes are for your business. You've got to figure that out. But I can walk you through the four skills you'll need that will give you the margin to make that happen and get you off that treadmill:

- Time management
- Delegation
- Budgeting
- Hiring

Keep in mind, you'll use these skills all the time and in every stage of business. But without the foundation for these skills, leveling up from Treadmill Operator to the next stage of business will be practically impossible.

TIME MANAGEMENT

You're successful. You've developed a service or product and a customer base. Great job! It's going well, but you're at your limit. Everyone who's winning will reach their limit at some point. That's why it's up to you to make sure you're spending every minute of your week on the right things. Time is the one resource that's truly fixed. We all have the same amount, and you can't get it back once it's gone.

So, are you spending most of your time working on things that are growing your business or on the ankle biters that get in the way? Until you take control of your time, you'll keep wondering where it all went, and you'll be left with only two options—working longer hours or working harder. And I know you. You already work your butt off, and you're already putting in long hours. But with three key time management tools, you can get a handle on where you're actually spending your time, start prioritizing your time more effectively, and finally stay on track with those priorities: the time audit, the time management matrix, and the forced ranking tasks exercise. Let's walk through how to put these tools to work.

Time Audit

As a busy leader, you're getting pulled in a hundred different directions, so you probably feel like everything is top priority. But the truth is, not everything has to happen right this minute. The time audit gives you the big-picture view of how you're spending your time today so you can start spending it on the right things going forward. The time audit is simple. Just jot down everything you do during the day over the course of a week. It works best if you track your time in thirty-minute increments in real time throughout the day. If you try to wait until the end of the day, you'll never remember what you did eight hours ago. Log every activity, even if you're just answering work texts and emails. Even on weekends.

I understand if you think this sounds like one more thing on your list that you have zero time for. But trust me, it's worth it. We worked with a guy who was running a construction company, and he was working at a jobsite about thirty minutes from his office. Out of habit, he was driving back to the office every day for lunch. That meant he was spending an hour each day—five hours a week—just driving back and forth for lunch! When his time audit showed him how much time he was wasting, it was an easy change for him to simply pack his lunch and skip the trip back to the office. That one change gave him back enough time to get his books done during the day instead of late at night after his family went to bed.

So, I bet you can spare a few seconds a few times a day to capture what you did for the last thirty minutes or so if it means getting back a few hours in your week. At the end of this chapter, we'll show you how to access our free Time Tracker Tool to make this step as quick and easy as possible.

Time Management Matrix

Once you have a good picture of where your week went, you have some decisions to make. You'll need to keep doing some things, stop some things, and delegate some things, which we'll talk about a little later. When I was figuring this out for myself, I liked using a tool that I first learned about in Stephen Covey's book *The 7 Habits of Highly Effective People*. He called it the Time Management Matrix, and it acts as a filter for all the activities you logged on your time audit.

URGENT   NOT URGENT

IMPORTANT

NOT IMPORTANT

Quadrant I: Urgent and Important—What has to be done now or it'll cause serious problems?

These tasks are usually easy to spot. Put every task from your time audit that's both important long term and urgent today in box number one. Urgent and Important stuff must be done immediately.

Quadrant 2: Important but Not Urgent—What do I need to work on to move my business and life to the next level but is not urgent?

Put all the tasks that are important long term but not urgent today into box number two. These are things you need to do, like exercise, strategic planning, goal setting, and date nights, and if you neglect these things for too long, they will become urgent. It's kind of like maintenance on your car. It's important to change the oil in your car, but if you don't do it regularly, you'll end up stranded on the side of the road with an urgent engine issue.

Quadrant 3: Urgent but Not Important—What am I doing simply because it's urgent that I should stop doing?

Put everything that's urgent today but not important long term into box number three. This includes things like, on a small scale, when a team member is standing in your doorway telling you that the copier is out of paper or, on a larger scale, when you're at risk of missing a deadline that could cause you to lose customers and money. Those are urgent tasks. Do them as soon as possible, but be careful! If the tyranny of the urgent wins out all the time, you'll end up focusing on the fire that will save $40 rather than the project that will generate $40,000.

Quadrant 4: Not Important and Not Urgent—What can I drop or delete?

These tasks should also be pretty easy to spot. They're your time wasters. This is stuff like watching television, scrolling social media, grabbing your phone every time it dings, or replying to the political email from your dumb-butt buddy. These are things that eat up valuable time but don't help you get anything done.

Seeing which quadrants get the biggest chunk of your time and energy changes the time-management game. Now you can focus your time on the tasks that are worth doing. Eventually, you'll start seeing patterns and learn to make better judgments about how you spend your time each day. That's huge for Treadmill Operators who are running full speed all day, every day.

Forced Ranking Tasks

You can organize your to-do list even further by using the forced ranking tasks exercise to prioritize the tasks you have to do in the short term so you can focus on the most important thing today. It's an easy way to identify your A1 activity, so I like to call this the steak sauce exercise. You can access the how-to for this and get a rundown of everything we've covered here in our Ultimate Guide to Time Management at the end of this chapter.

DELEGATION

As the owner of your small business, how much do you think your time is worth? Two hundred dollars an hour? Three hundred? More? Now think about how much it would cost you to hire an assistant. Someone to answer the phones, handle paperwork, manage your schedule, and take notes in meetings. About $20 an hour? If I offered you a $20 bill in exchange for $200, you'd have no problem telling me what a bad deal that is. But that's effectively what you're doing every hour you spend at $200 a pop on tasks someone else could be doing for $20 an hour. Not only that, but those tasks are also taking up your time and keeping you from working on your business and growing revenue. I'm not saying those tasks aren't important. You might not think twice about doing them yourself, and you may even enjoy them. But you're shortchanging yourself when you don't delegate them to someone else.

Delegation is one of the most misunderstood and abused areas of leadership in small businesses today. It's not just blindly pushing your responsibilities off onto another team member. Effective delegation starts with a detailed description and explanation of why you want to delegate a task to a team member. Your team member needs to know why the task is important, how it relates to their role, and how much time you expect them to spend on it. When you delegate the right way, you activate your team members to work in their personal strengths on particular tasks, and that, in turn, frees you up to focus on other tasks only you can do.

If you're thinking that sounds like a lot of work, you're right. And that's one excuse small-business leaders use to avoid delegation. I've heard plenty more excuses and even had a bunch of my own. Does any of this ring a bell?

"It takes too long to teach somebody else."

"Nobody can do the task as well as I can."

"I still like doing the task."

"I can't risk losing control."

When you get down to it, there are really two main reasons why business owners don't delegate: Either they don't have the people they need, or they have the people on their team, but they aren't trained. The first problem—not having the right people on the team—is solved through hiring. We'll talk about what a good hiring process looks like later, but when you're looking to build a team of people you can delegate to, you want to look for two specific character traits: integrity and competency.

Psychologist and *New York Times* bestselling author Dr. Henry Cloud explains that the word *integrity* comes from the root word *integer*. An integer is any whole number, not a fraction. In life, integrity means living in wholeness—no splits or hypocrisy. It's being the same person with the same general behavior in any setting. Look for positive team members who model consistency no matter how much time you spend with them.

When it comes to competency, you're looking for more than the ability to accomplish the task. Competency is about *how* the task is accomplished. Cloud says, "Character is the ability to meet the demands of reality." People with the character to be delegation-worthy are mature enough to know their limitations, they know when to ask for help, and they consistently show a level of excellence and the diligence to maintain it. They're also courageous enough to bring you bad news when it's called for without hiding anything, even if it reflects badly on them.

Business owners can solve the second problem—lack of training—by simply taking the time to train the people they do have. Some leaders are hesitant about training because they don't want to be micromanagers. Showing people how things need to be done is *not* micromanaging; it's training. Once you've trained your team member and they've proven they can do the task, but you continue to hover over their shoulder, *that's* micromanaging.

Delegation is a critical strategy for growth. Even if you use every minute of every hour of every day well, your business will grow only as big as your ability to delegate. It's up to you to push past the excuses if you want to grow your business beyond the Treadmill Operator stage. At first, delegation will be one of the hardest things you'll do in business. But if you slow down to master the delegation process now, you'll be set to speed up later. I dive deep into this process in detail in my Quick Read brilliantly titled *Delegation*, which you'll also be able to access at the end of the chapter.

BUDGETING

I can't stress enough how important a budget is to running your business. That shouldn't be a shock coming from the guy who teaches people how to handle their money. You need to know where your business stands financially at all times. Your budget will show you that and help you generate the margin you need to grow your business. A budget is a plan for your money (what you make, spend, and save) where you tell your money (aka revenue) where to go. Think of your budget as a windshield that lets you see what's coming up and gauge how you're doing on reaching your destination.

In the Treadmill Operator stage, the biggest benefit of having a budget is that it will show you if you can or can't afford to hire help to grow your business. If you don't make enough money to hire help, then you need to figure out how to make more money. Your business budget will make that clear, show you where you might be able to make adjustments, and help you problem solve for how you can afford to hire more team members.

You also shouldn't be surprised that a guy who preaches about staying out of debt in life also believes you should stay out of debt in business. Really. Just like living debt-free in your personal life is countercultural, running a debt-free business is totally and completely countercultural. But it can be done. People are shocked when they learn that we built our fifty-acre, $400 million headquarters without debt. Regardless, it's true. We don't borrow money. I continually remind our team that we build (and grow) at the speed of cash. You can too, and that starts with a solid budgeting process.

At first, you'll focus on your budget for the next month and work your way up to a projected twelve- to eighteen-month budget. As you do that, you'll create retained earnings, which is the secret to staying out of debt in business. Imagine being able to see where your business could be financially a year from now. How much better would you be able to plan and take advantage of the opportunities that come your way with that kind of knowledge? This is why budgeting is an essential skill for Treadmill Operators who are ready to break into the next stage of business.

Of course, you'll need some practical, tactical guidance to build a budget for your business for the first time. Again, we'll give you access to the whole step-by-step process plus a few pro tips we've learned along the way at the end of the chapter. What's really important right now is that you understand the value a budget will bring to your business and your life so that you put in the effort to build that skill and put it into action. If you do, this time next month, my bet is you'll have a whole new outlook on your business!

HIRING

Once you've optimized your time, worked on delegating some tasks to others, and built your operating budget, you're ready to grow your business. Things are starting to move, and that's a good thing. But the only way to solve the problem of having more work than you can get done is to hire more team members. When you have good help, you can continue to focus on growing the business, not just running it. Good hires keep your business moving forward.

Your first hire is a huge step. It's a big investment financially, and at this stage, when your business is so small, just one crazy person can really screw things up! As much as you need the help, I promise you a bad hire is worse than no hire. When I started adding team members, I'd hire someone if they could just fog a mirror. I thought if I hired them to work, they would actually work. Wrong! There are a lot of people out there just looking for a J-O-B so they can collect a paycheck. You don't want those people on your team.

Hiring the right person is more important than hiring a person. Again, another lesson I learned the hard way.

So, even though you need help now—yesterday would have been better—my advice to you is to slow down. In his book *Good to Great*, my friend Jim Collins talks about the importance of getting the right people in the right seats on the bus. To do that, you need to take your time. The hiring mistakes I made early on showed me the value of having a good hiring process. Ours has twelve—yes, twelve—components we refined over time. When we follow it (we still aren't perfect), we have a great batting average on hiring great team members.

The Twelve Components to a Good Hire

1. Pray.

   Ask God to send the team members you need to do the work He's given you to do and keep out the crazy. If prayer is not your thing, at least take some time to nail down the type of person you want (and don't want) to work with every day. Reflection brings clarity.

2. Get referrals.

   Thoroughbreds run with thoroughbreds, so ask your team members to refer people from their circle who they'd want to work with. If their referral is hired and completes the ninety-day probation period, give the referring team member a cash bounty—and hand it out in front of the entire team. There's nothing like a little cash to inspire great leads and build culture at the same time!

3. Do a thirty-minute drive-by interview.

   Never—I repeat, never—hire someone after just one interview. Start with a thirty-minute get-to-know-you conversation where they do most of the talking while you ask questions and listen. Make sure that first call (phone or video) doesn't go over thirty minutes. You'll be amazed at what you learn in that call, and you'll be clear on whether to set up a second interview.

4. Check the resumés and references.

   A resumé gives you an overview of the candidate's formal training, skills, and certifications. Use it as a conversation starter, but don't lean on it (or on their references) too much. People can say anything. Occasionally, when you check a reference, you'll find a candidate didn't tell them to expect a call or email. The candidate may even include someone who doesn't have nice things to say. These are often signals to run in the opposite direction.

5. Use testing tools.

You need enough relational intelligence to know who to bring on, but the right tools can also help you figure out if someone would be a good fit in the role. You might give a skills test to candidates for roles in writing, copy editing, presenting, design, or web development so you can see if they have the chops to do the job. Another fit indicator is the DISC assessment. It'll give you a quick look at how the candidate's style of behavior, communication, and work fit the team and the work you need done. For example, if you need someone great at crunching numbers, you would ideally want to see high scores in organization and details (the C) on their assessment. If you don't, that could spark additional questions about how that works for them.

6. Ask yourself, do you like them?

Hire people you like. It's that simple. You run a small business and probably spend a lot of time with your team, so relationships matter. Skills alone aren't enough. If someone's good at the task but they're a jerk or have a vastly different value system, you won't like working with them (and they won't like working with you either). Plus, your customers probably won't like interacting with them. That's never good.

7. Look for passion. (Do they light up?)

Look for passion when they talk about the position and your company's mission. Lack of passion is the easiest way to spot someone just looking for a J-O-B. If all they want is a paycheck, you'll never keep them happy. You want team members who are excited about what they're doing—construction workers who want to build homes for families to make memories in, writers who want to inspire hope, and web developers who want to create a fantastic experience for customers. Look for fired-up people who love their work and own the *why* behind it.

8. Review their personal budget.

Can the candidate afford to live on the salary you provide? If not, sooner or later, they'll blame you for "not paying enough" even though they accepted your offer and should know what they can and can't live on. When people are worried about their bills, they're distracted and can't give their best. So serve your top candidates—before they join you—by making sure they can care for their family and meet their obligations with what you pay. Make it clear that you're not going to scrutinize their budget to see where they spend their money; this is just another way to make sure this is a good fit.

9. Discuss compensation.

Notice that this comes further down the process than many people expect. That's okay. It makes sense for people to want to know what the compensation package is, so share it with them once you've made it a bit further into the hiring process. If their first question during one of the initial interviews is about how much you're going to pay them, they'll leave you for ten cents more an hour. They're takers, not givers. You want people excited to add value to your organization. If they're preoccupied by the benefits, don't hire them.

10. Create a Key Results Area (KRA).

A KRA is a written roadmap for what winning looks like in the role you're filling. A KRA can be as simple as defining the number of calls and sales volume required of a sales position or the maximum time a customer should be on hold. Operating without a KRA is like taking people bowling without the lights on. They'll make a lot of noise but won't really know what they're doing. That's why you need to be clear about the role you're hiring for—otherwise, the person you hire could leave when they find out what their job really is. Don't set a new team member up for failure by not being clear about what you expect them to do. We'll talk a lot more about KRAs and how to create them for your team members in the next chapter.

11. Do a final in-person interview and go on a spousal dinner.

This may be the best advice on the list. This is one of the final checks on whether a potential team member will be a great fit. A spousal dinner is your chance to get to know the candidate and their spouse while you share your company story in a casual restaurant setting. It's a game changer. As their spouse hears about your culture and the role, they're usually eager to share whether they think the position fits. One more bonus: You'll discover if your candidate is married to crazy. If they are, stay away. Seriously.

12. Implement a ninety-day onboarding and probation plan.

    Once a person is hired, they start out on a probation period—we use ninety days—so everyone can make sure the fit is right. This is a low-obligation period where they can walk away if they choose. But if they decide to leave, discuss what went wrong and try to fix it first. You've invested a lot to get to this point. Every quarter or so, celebrate all your new team members who made it through their first ninety days. This is the perfect time for you and your leaders to pass the baton to them as creators of your company culture. At Ramsey Solutions, we invite these new team members to a special celebration at the end of a workday. We provide a meal, I talk about how we got started, I let some of our other leaders share, and then I allow these new team members to ask questions. It's a great time to celebrate them while also reinforcing our culture.

What Winning Looks Like

I don't know about you, but when I zoom out and look at all that's in this chapter, it's a lot. Honestly, when I think back to when I was on the treadmill, not only was my day-to-day workload unsustainable but also having to think about doing all this stuff on top of that was overwhelming. What they say is true, though: "The thinking that got us into this problem isn't the thinking that's going to get us out of it." To grow your business, you'll have to learn new skills and think differently about how you spend your time. I've seen what happens when Treadmill Operators don't make those changes. They stay stuck and frequently burn out. Just as bad, many of them fall short of their dreams and never have much impact. And of course, we've all heard the statistics about how many small businesses go under every year. You have to stop letting your business run you and start running your business. I believe in the inherent nobility of business, and I believe in you, the EntreLeader. Because there's heart in what you do. You're more than the renegade lone ranger or the corporate bureaucrat. And I want to see you win at business and have a blast doing it.

If you'll put in the work to master the four skills we've covered in this chapter, you'll get to the point where most of the business results don't rely on you personally generating them. Here they are again:

- Time management
- Delegation
- Budgeting
- Hiring

You'll know you're conquering this stage when you consistently have time each week to work *on* the business, not just *in* it. You'll be thinking about where you want the business to be in the future, working on longer-range goals like improving your marketing—and all the other things on your to-do list that you never have time to get to today. You'll finally have time to think about how to make your business work better, and not just react to the most recent fire.

The biggest shift will happen when you can afford to hire team members you can delegate to, and you can trust that the work will get done in a way that you are proud of. This is the difference between owning a job and owning a business—the ability to scale. You'll scale your impact. You'll break free from the treadmill because you've imposed your will on the challenges of the marketplace while still making it home for dinner with your family. That's what winning looks like, and that's what will move you to the next stage of business, Pathfinder.

Scan the QR code below to get a comprehensive step-by-step action plan with tools and resources that will help you create margin in your day so you can spend time working *on* your business instead of just *in* it.

Client Success Story

Sam and Kaoma Massa, HiViz Lighting, Inc.

Sam and Kaoma Massa run HiViz Lighting, Inc., in Hendersonville, North Carolina, and they're a great example of a company that worked through the Treadmill Operator stage. Their primary business is to provide high-quality LED light bars and light assemblies for emergency vehicles and first responders. Their mission is to save lives by providing reliable lighting technologies that make it possible for first responders to work more safely and effectively after dark. They're so passionate about what they do that Sam still works part time with fire/rescue/ EMS in their community.

Almost as soon as Sam began working as a first responder, he noticed a distinct need for specialty lighting that would help people in that field be even better, and safer, at their jobs.

"One night, while on a call, the ambulance kept going past the house we were at because they couldn't see the addresses well enough," Sam explained. "I never want a first responder to have to wonder if they have the right gear to help save someone's life. So we started HiViz Lighting, Inc., with the goal to revolutionize the way fire and emergency services personnel do their jobs after dark so they can save more lives."

HiViz Lighting got its start in 2011 from Sam and Kaoma's small home office and even smaller workshop. At the time, Sam was only making $10 an hour working night shifts with the fire department. During the day, he created and built special lights and brackets as one-offs for local fire departments and utility companies, hustling for every order he could get.

"When it became apparent that Sam needed help with bookkeeping and scheduling, I would do that during my lunch hour at my regular job," Kaoma explained. "Sam is more of a start-now-plan-later type, and I'm more of the plan-now-start-later type, so we have a nice balance."

The budget was so tight in those early days, they couldn't afford to buy boxes to ship their orders in, so Sam would go to the local hardware store and take any empty boxes they had for free. Then, when he shipped them to his customers, he added a sticker for just a penny each that said, "We care about the environment, so we're using recycled boxes."

"All of that was gritty and fun with just the two of us," Kaoma shared, "but it was also unsustainable."

Within a few short years, their company had taken off, and sales were pouring in. But without a team, structure, or plan, Sam and Kaoma knew they couldn't maintain the rapid pace.

"We were totally winging it and doing everything on our own," Kaoma said. "We knew our business would plateau if we didn't do something different."

When Sam and Kaoma found EntreLeadership, HiViz Lighting was a $4 million company. Clearly, they were doing a lot of things right, and they used what they learned from EntreLeadership to pour gasoline on those areas. At the same time, they followed the EntreLeadership System to focus on the areas that needed improvement—like hiring the right people (and firing the wrong people). With the courage and confidence that they were making the right decisions, they got to work building the team they desperately needed.

Then COVID-19 hit. At the time, Sam and Kaoma were traveling almost three hundred days a year to trade shows to reach new potential customers, and the shutdown meant all those trade shows were canceled. That could have been a disaster for them, but they turned it into an opportunity.

"The break in travel allowed us to focus on our core business systems and principles," Kaoma explained. "And since we weren't traveling, we saved a huge amount of money that we would have otherwise spent."

And they didn't stop there. Sam had another creative solution up his sleeve.

"We took a lot of that money and built a state-of-the-art video studio that allowed us to reach out to customers digitally from a professional space," Sam said. "While our competitors were doing Zoom calls with terrible lighting and bad audio, we were hosting weekly, live, online, highly produced training events that looked and sounded great."

That investment in quality and the customer experience differentiated HiViz Lighting from its competitors, and customers noticed. "Our business exploded during that time," Sam said.

While Sam and Kaoma projected only 25 percent growth for 2021 due to the uncertainties of the pandemic, they actually experienced a 50 percent increase in revenue that year! Part of that was due to excellent planning. They got ahead of supply chain issues by increasing inventory early in 2020. With enough inventory to fill orders through 2022, they were in a position to add team members during a time when most companies were letting team members go.

"We added fifteen new rock stars to our team using the hiring system we learned from EntreLeadership," Kaoma said.

Now, HiViz Lighting is a $25 million company that provides solutions for 60 percent of the lighting in fire apparatus in the country. They also provide emergency lighting solutions to countries around the globe and only have a 10 percent failure rate—the best in the industry.

"Sometimes I miss those early, gritty days, even though they were hard in their own way," Kaoma said. "But now, I get to pick and choose the things I want to work on. Building a great team means I can now work on the business versus in it, and I can focus on the parts I really enjoy! That's a reward for pushing through the Treadmill Operator stage!"

STAGE

2

PATHFINDER

KEY CHALLENGE:

You lack clear direction.

WHAT WINNING LOOKS LIKE:

Your team is engaged in a shared direction.

PATHFINDER

Have you ever had that feeling that something is wrong, but you can't put your finger on it? It's a strange, unsettling feeling you get in your spirit. That happened to me around the time we were moving out of the Treadmill Operator stage. We were starting to get the radio show into some new markets, and *Financial Peace University* was just coming out on video. Everything was moving in the right direction, and I was excited to see that forward momentum. But the air in the building didn't have the right energy. There was something dark and lingering, but as a young, inexperienced leader, I couldn't understand where it was coming from. Then one morning, I stumbled right into the source of the sludge we were stuck in.

I'd just wrapped up our weekly staff meeting. We had about twelve team members then, and we held our staff meeting around a big conference table. I left for an appointment right after the meeting, but when I got out to my car, I realized I'd left my keys inside. As I walked back through the door, I could hear my top salesperson talking. She had her back to the door, and the rest of the team was still in the conference room, listening as she conducted the "meeting after the meeting," like they do in corporate America. She was ripping me to shreds and telling my team that the business would never get anywhere because I was such a terrible leader. I stood there, completely floored by what I was hearing.

The team could see me standing behind her, but no one stopped her. She just kept digging that hole deeper and deeper until, finally, I guess the hair on the back of her neck stood up and she turned around and literally said, "Oh, crap."

"Well, I reckon we're done, aren't we?" I said. She followed me to my office, and when we got there, she had the nerve to act surprised when I told her she was done working for me.

"Done? What do you mean?"

"You don't work here anymore," I said. "Either you're an idiot or I'm an idiot—or we're both idiots. Because if you're so dumb that you will work for a person you think is an idiot, that makes you an idiot. And if I'm so dumb that I keep paying somebody who thinks I'm an idiot, that makes me an idiot. So apparently, we're both idiots in this story, but at least we're not going to be idiots together anymore."

I knew it was the right thing to do, but she was popular with the team—our top salesperson, for crying out loud. I wasn't sure how the team would react to my firing her. It was like that epic moment in *The Wizard of Oz* where the Wicked Witch and her cossack-looking soldiers with their big, furry hats and curved swords have Dorothy and her friends cornered in the witch's castle. The Wicked Witch uses her broom to set Scarecrow on fire, and Dorothy grabs a bucket of water to put out the fire and save her friend. But some of the water splashes onto the Wicked Witch, and apparently, you can't throw water on witches, because she melts right in front of them. When there's nothing left of her but a steaming hat and cloak, there's this theatrical, pregnant pause. The Wicked Witch's soldiers are all looking at Dorothy, and you think for an instant they're going to turn their curved swords on her because she just killed their boss. Instead, they suddenly kneel down in front of her and shout, "Hail to Dorothy. The Wicked Witch is dead!"

That's what happened when I told the team I'd fired our toxic top salesperson. Well, not the kneeling down part, but definitely the part where they all felt a sense of relief. Number one because the source of all that bad energy was gone. And number two, they'd seen that I was a leader who wouldn't tolerate bull crap. That I actually had a spine and wouldn't let someone poison the team with gossip just because they were the top salesperson and I was too big of a coward to get rid of them.

That decision not only built a ton of trust with my team but was also a huge step toward defining the type of business we would become. It was our declaration that we wouldn't put up with backstabbing corporate nonsense, and we would operate based on principle. We still had a lot of work to do to get all that nailed down, of course, but every business that wins has to engage in the process of defining itself and then communicate that to its team and customers. And that process is what defines the Pathfinder stage of business.

Herding Cats

If the Treadmill Operator stage is about taking your business from your doing everything by yourself to your leading a team that gets the work done and brings in the revenue, then the Pathfinder stage is about creating the clarity and alignment you and your team need to do that well. At this stage, your business might be making money, but it feels a bit (or a lot) messy. You'll fix one problem, only to see another pop up, like a game of Whac-A-Mole. Team members don't stick around, because they're not really bought in to the business and what you're trying to achieve. And the biggest issue is that it feels like no one really understands or cares as much as the Pathfinder does about the business's goals and values. It's like trying to steer a ship where not everyone is rowing in the same direction or, worse, some don't even know why they're on the boat.

Pathfinders also struggle with the fact that they're not as busy doing the hands-on work that gave them their start. They used to be the hero who made the kill and dragged it back to the cave, but now their main job is to figure out what the business should do next. They might even have more money than they ever thought they would, which is cool, but that also leads to a lot of questions. Like, when is the right time to hire more people? And what should those new team members do? Those are tough questions to answer when everything is growing so fast and it's so hard to plan for the future.

It's lonely and disappointing when you have a team that doesn't get what your business is about. It's like being excited for a group project only to find that no one else shares your vision or enthusiasm. That causes a lot of business owners to question their own leadership abilities. They thought that by bringing people on board, the journey would become easier and more fulfilling. Instead, it feels like they're spending all their time and energy herding a bunch of cats.

SIGNS YOU MAY BE IN THE PATHFINDER STAGE

Team member turnover is high.

You have unreliable results.

The team doesn't demonstrate the values that created your initial success.

The team is not aligned.

FRUSTRATIONS YOU FACE IN THE PATHFINDER STAGE

You're used to putting out fires, and you feel uncomfortable about being "not needed" now that you've delegated some of those responsibilities.

You're unsure about how to spend your time—it's a big shift from leaving the cave, killing something, and dragging it home. Now the team is doing that.

You're making more money than you ever have before, and you don't know how to invest in the business.

You're not alone if you're dealing with these issues in the Pathfinder stage. It's actually very normal. We've heard business owners who are in the Pathfinder stage ask questions like:

"My business is growing faster than I ever planned on. Where do I go next?"

"How do I know when it's the right time to hire more people? What roles should they be in?"

"How do I get the team aligned and all pointed at the same goals?"

Don't get the wrong idea. The Pathfinder stage is exciting. Your business is doing well and is on a trajectory to do even better. But growth and opportunity come with challenges. And as much as you'd like someone to swoop in and just tell you what to do, you've got to lead your business through those challenges. I have no doubt you can do that once you know what to focus on. I'll point you in the right direction based on the steps we took at Ramsey Solutions and how we've coached thousands of other businesses as they've worked their way through the Pathfinder stage.

Finding True North

The solution to getting all those cats you've been herding to line up and head in the same direction at the same time is to get your team on the same page. It's a simple concept, but that doesn't mean it's easy! The Pathfinder must shift from completing tasks and solving problems to truly leading the team toward a common goal. They need to identify and share their overall vision for the business and then make sure everyone understands and cares about it. And that's practically impossible without these components:

- Mission statement
- Vision
- Core values
- Role clarity
- Clear communication

These elements of business are all about creating clarity and alignment for your business and your team. The day I fired the salesperson who was gossiping behind my back, we developed a core value. The No Gossip rule was our stake in the ground: We would not be a company that gossiped. And to this day, all our team members, old and new, are aligned with that expectation.

When you do the work to establish and communicate these components for your business, you'll make the leap from being hyperfocused on day-to-day stuff to thinking about the big picture and how to grow the business in a good way. And I'll be honest, this stage is tough because it requires you to have a whole new mindset about your business, but it's also an exciting chance to make your business stronger and more united.

MISSION STATEMENT

When it comes to small-business failure, the number one cause is not having enough money. And the number two cause is too much success. Really. A business that bills itself as "a tire repair, hair care, and airports services business" could actually be good at all those things. It could even be successful at making money doing those things. But it won't get any real traction until it defines the kind of business it truly is—by first defining the kind of business it is not. Your company's mission statement is an out-of-bounds marker that helps you know what you are not.

When you started your business, you had a purpose, and it was probably enough to just have that purpose in your head. Especially if you were the one doing all the work. But once other people get involved, your mission has to become bigger than simply making payroll by Friday. It has to be something that inspires the entire team. Your company's mission statement defines the heart and soul of your business. It answers the questions "Who are we?" and "Why do we exist?"

In his book *Start with Why*, Simon Sinek talks about how important it is to know the *why* behind what you do. It's what inspires people and makes them believe in your cause. That's why a mission statement isn't just a bunch of fancy words that look and sound nice on your website. It needs to capture the reason you and your team get up to come to work in the morning. When you create a mission statement, you find that *why* for your business, and when you get it right, your mission statement will be foundational to your business for a long time.

I'll confess, I wasn't super excited all those years ago to take the time to create a mission statement. It was a lot of hard work to try to put words to who we are and why we're in business. We filled a trash can with crumpled-up attempts. It took over a month of prayer, work, and frustration to gradually form clear answers to those questions that would hold up in the decades to come. The cool thing is that now, thirty-plus years later, we still operate on that same mission statement with just one minor change. That says to us that we built a good one and that we have stayed true to our calling. Our mission statement is:

Ramsey Solutions provides biblically based, commonsense education and empowerment that give hope to everyone in every walk of life.

Short and sweet, but it captures the heartbeat of Ramsey Solutions. Here are some other recognizable companies and their mission statements:

Apple: To challenge the status quo. To think differently.

Coca-Cola: To refresh the world and inspire moments of optimism and happiness.

Facebook: To give people the power to build community so that we can bring the world closer together.

Microsoft: To empower every person and organization on the planet to achieve more.

Harley-Davidson: To fulfill dreams of personal, all-American freedom.

Google: To organize the world's information and make it universally accessible and useful.

Disney: To create happiness for people of all ages, everywhere.

Tesla: To accelerate the world's transition to sustainable energy.

Starbucks: To inspire and nurture the human spirit—one person and one cup at a time.

Amazon: To be Earth's most customer-centric company.

Toyota, USA: To attract and attain customers with high-valued products and services and the most satisfying ownership experience in America.

McDonald's: To make delicious feel-good moments easy for everyone.

If you nail this for your business, you'll inspire not only yourself but everyone around you too. So find that *why*, make it super clear, and let it light the way for your business. Start by asking yourself some questions like:

- What is the big passion that drives everyone in our company?
- What are the skills and abilities that set us apart?
- What are the personality traits of our business?
- What is the good our company does for the community or the world, and how do we accomplish what we do?

As you think through these questions, jot down whatever answers come to mind without overthinking it and use those thoughts to sum up the purpose of your business in just a few words. How would you say it in a way that feels true to you? As you draft different versions, aim for your mission statement to be:

- Short enough for your team to remember and repeat easily
- Really simple
- Big and bold
- Something that makes people go, "Oh, wow!"
- Straight from the heart
- Bigger, more long term than just a goal

You won't hit all these points on your first try, and that's fine. Just see what's missing, and keep working on it. Keep polishing it. When you feel like it's close, ask yourself: *Does this really speak to me? Is this why we're doing all this hard work? Does it make me want to jump out of bed in the morning?*

In the end, you want a short statement (not a story) that nails down what your business is all about. And keep in mind, words matter, so choose words that mean something to you. Whatever you do, though, don't resort to generic, corporate mumbo jumbo. This is about defining the heart of your business so that it beats strong for everyone to hear and follow. Choose powerful, specific words that will light up your whole team—something they can believe in and get excited about.

This is a big step for you as a leader. You've probably never had to think at this level about your business and why it exists. At the end of this chapter, you'll get access to our Mission Statement Builder that will walk you through the steps to build a mission statement you and your whole team can rally around now and into the future.

VISION

Proverbs 29:18 says, "Where there is no vision, the people perish" (KJV). I don't know about you, but I can't think of a better reason to create and cast a compelling vision for your team than that. Without a vision, people perish! Now, we're not talking about your team actually dying here, but without a vision, your business will start to fall apart. Morale tanks, people start dragging their feet, turnover rates shoot up, sales plummet, and before you know it, you're scrambling just to keep the lights on.

If you're like most business leaders, *having* a vision isn't the problem. Business leaders are visionaries who see a world of possibility others don't. It's your superpower. But until you help your team understand and get excited about where you're going, they can't help you get there. That's the job of your vision statement.

Now, if you're scratching your head, wondering what the difference is between a mission statement and a vision statement, let me clear that up for you. While your mission statement answers the questions "Who are we?" and "Why do we exist?," your vision statement paints a picture of what the world would look like if you were 100 percent successful in fulfilling your mission. It defines where your business is going and what its impact in the world will be.

Ramsey Solutions' vision statement is:

We see a world in which so many lives are radically transformed, the toxic culture is disrupted.

It answers the questions "Where is Ramsey Solutions going?" and "What will it look like when we live out our mission?" But that's not where our vision started. Many years ago, before Ramsey Solutions was even a thing, I went for a walk with a yellow pad and pencil in hand. I started dreaming on paper. I had a vision for the coming years for how many radio stations we'd be on and how many people would be going through FPU all across the country. Was I dreaming? Well, kind of, yes, but I was also developing a vision for where I wanted to take my business. I wrote down what I believed it could one day become. I had most of that in my head already, but writing it down and sharing it with my team was electric. It fired people up. It gave them a North Star.

So, how do you develop a vision statement? A long walk with a yellow notepad is a good start. In fact, getting out of the office is practically a must for you to have the time (aim for at least an hour) and focus to do this right. Start by writing down your answers to these questions:

- What problem do you want solved for your customer?
- What do you want customers to experience?
- What do you want to be known and trusted for?
- What do you want your business to be, to have, or to do long term?

While your vision statement is huge for inspiring and aligning your team, it's also personal to you. If you're feeling stuck, try thinking about your own internal motivations.

What did you dream of becoming when you were a kid? How does that relate to what you're doing now? What's driving you, or, better yet, what makes you angry enough to keep working toward change in your community or industry? That will help you connect the work you're doing to the impact you want your business to have in the world.

Like you did with your mission statement, use your answers to draft a vision statement. Then keep refining it until you've got a short, inspiring, and clear vision statement your team can latch on to and run with. You'll find that when your team understands how their work fits into the big picture, they bring a new level of passion and drive for excellence. And don't be surprised if you start to see your vision statement affect your bottom line too. A recent nationwide survey of employees by Gallup shows that just making your team feel 10 percent more connected to the company's purpose can drop turnover rates by over 8 percent and boost profits by 4.4 percent. That's huge!

So, what's the takeaway? Lead with a vision. It's that simple. It's like giving your team a road map and a reason to get excited about the journey. Plus, it just makes everything a whole lot more fun and meaningful.

CORE VALUES

You've done a lot of soul-searching already to get your mission and vision nailed down. I told you it would be hard work, and you've still got more to do. So now seems like a good time to remind you to trust the process. It will all start coming together soon, and like other businesses that have gone through this before you, including Ramsey Solutions, you'll see the hard work pay off as you see more unity and alignment on your team. Sounds too good to be true, I know. But it's the only thing that makes this kind of work worth it in the end.

Now you're ready to start identifying your core values. These are the deep-rooted convictions that define how you do business and set you apart from your competitors. They tell your team what's expected of them, and they tell the world what you stand for. Together with your mission and vision statements, your core values guide you as you make decisions about everything from the next business initiative you pursue to how you handle a team member's last-minute time-off request. Based on our own experience, the best core values are not aspirational. In other words,

Ramsey Solutions' core values don't describe who we *want* to be, they describe who we *are*. They are the foundation of our company culture, and we expect all our team members to be aligned with them.

Ramsey Solutions Core Values

Colossians 3:23: We do our work as unto the Lord.

Crusade: We are crusaders doing work that matters.

Excellence in the Ordinary: We are faithful in the little things.

Family: We balance family and working hard.

Fear Not: We don't make decisions based on fear.

Marketplace Service: If we help enough people, we don't have to worry about money.

Momentum Theorem: We know that focused intensity over time, multiplied by God, equals unstoppable momentum.

Never Give Up: We impose our will on the marketplace.

No Gossip: We pass negatives up and positives all around.

Righteous Living: We believe character matters. All the time.

Self-Employed Mentality: We all care and take responsibility like we own the place.

Share the Profits: We win together. We lose together.

Shoot Sacred Cows: We stick by our principles. We challenge traditions.

Team: We are team members, not employees.

This is what our core values look like today after several iterations over time. Rick Perry, my very first HR hire, put together the original version of our core values after watching me and my key leaders at the time make decisions about the business, about people issues—whatever we had to deal with. He noticed patterns in the choices we made and pointed out that we were using specific principles—core values—we should document. While we didn't follow a specific process to do that then, today we have identified a few steps that will help you replicate, in a more focused, streamlined way, the progression of our core values so you can get yours right the first time.

Six Steps to Create Your Core Values

1. Identify your personal core values.

   As the owner, your business is built around your vision and mission. Your personal beliefs will affect your business, which means your personal and business values need to line up. Ask yourself: *What do I stand for? What values would I like to live out but I'm not actually achieving? What does success look like to me?*

2. Brainstorm with your key leaders.

Bring in your leadership team and decide together how to weave your personal values into your business. With their buy-in, you can share your core values as a unified force. If you don't have leaders to share your values with yet, bring your spouse, a mentor, or a trusted team member into the conversation.

3. Observe.

How do you and your team function when you're at your best? What words or phrases describe the things that set your company and culture apart from others? What are some things that are important to your team members? What kinds of things have you seen shaping your team culture? Get specific about what makes your business unique.

4. List your nonnegotiables.

What do you refuse to compromise on? These are the hard things you're willing to lose business over, like setting certain business hours or refusing to work with vendors with shady practices (no matter how low their prices are). These are the principles that ultimately set your business apart and attract your most loyal, like-minded tribe.

5. Refine the list.

At this point, you'll have a pretty long list of words and phrases that describe your company. Narrow it down by choosing quality over quantity. There's no right or wrong number of core values to have, but keep it to a number that's easy for you and your team to remember. We have a lot of core values. In fact, my friend Pat Lencioni was leading an off-site with my operating board and observed that we have fourteen core values. He and I got into a fun argument with him saying, by definition, fourteen is not "core." He said we had too many "core" values. He might be right that fewer is better, but we like ours, so for our purposes, we're keeping them. But don't feel like you have to mimic our list. We did what we felt was right for our business, and you'll need to do what's right for yours.

6.   Make them sticky.

You'll be talking about your core values all the time, practically reciting them in your sleep. So make sure the wording represents your company exactly the way you want it to be.

Like your mission and vision statements, your core values aren't just pretty words to post on your website and forget about. You have to integrate them into how you do business, and you do that by keeping them front and center with your team. At Ramsey, we cover our core values as part of our hiring process so candidates can ask questions and understand our expectations before they join the team. We talk about them again in new team member onboarding, and we display our core values throughout our campus so the team never has to wonder how vital they are to the way we work.

ROLE CLARITY

When your team is small, everyone wears a lot of different hats. It's the only way to get all the work done. But as your team grows, so does the need to get clear on who is responsible for what. Think of it like being the coach of a basketball team. You want each player to know their position and how they can score points for the team. That's role clarity.

I mentioned KRAs (Key Results Areas) back in the hiring process section. At Ramsey Solutions, we create role clarity with KRAs for every person in the building. Our KRAs have come a long way since I talked about them in my book *EntreLeadership*. But the idea behind the KRA is still the same. A KRA is a written description of what winning looks like in a team member's role. The team member works with their leader to develop their KRA, then both of them sign it, leaving no room for confusion about what the team member should be working on. KRAs empower team members to take personal responsibility and ownership for the work they are doing.

Here's what our KRAs look like: Short and simple—KRAs are best kept to one page. Otherwise, your team member ends up with too many things to work on to be effective. At the end of this chapter, you'll get access to a five-minute video that will walk you through how to fill out a KRA and provide an editable KRA template so you can see how easy this is to do yourself.

Putting KRAs to Work

Creating KRAs for all your team members is the first step toward role clarity. To really make them effective, you have to get intentional about holding team members accountable to their KRAs. At Ramsey, we do that with weekly one-on-one meetings between team members and their leaders where team members can ask questions, bring up any blockers, and get help from their leaders to remove those blockers. One-on-ones are also opportunities for leaders to coach up their team members on hard and soft skills so they're always growing in their role and in their ability to take on new responsibilities.

Remember, too, that KRAs are living, breathing documents. Team members' focus areas will change as the business needs change. So leaders need to re-evaluate their team's KRAs at least a couple of times a year to see if they need to make any adjustments. Again, the leader and team member work on those changes together, and they both sign off, eliminating any potential confusion.

Are you starting to see how the pieces we've talked about come together to create a crystal clear direction for your company and your team? You're defining your company's purpose and direction and showing your team exactly how they fit into that to keep the company moving forward. But it's not enough to put all these concepts into words. Now you've got to go all in on an all-out, never-ending communication campaign with your team.

CLEAR COMMUNICATION

If you read *EntreLeadership*, you know I spent an entire chapter of that book talking about the importance of communication. It is absolutely essential that the right hand knows what the left hand is doing if you're going to keep fear and distrust from taking over your business. Companies that win are intentional about building a culture of communication, and *EntreLeadership* covers all the ways we did that at Ramsey Solutions, much of it as we progressed through our Pathfinder stage. It's interesting to look back and see that we're still using all those same methods today.

The foundation of that culture is overcommunication. We talk about the good things as well as the bad things all the time—with all our team members. Why? Because we're all adults, and we treat our team like adults. We know that if we don't communicate or if we communicate poorly, the team will fill in the blanks for themselves. And because it's human nature to assume the worst, they'll create a scenario in their minds that's ten times worse than reality. No team on earth can be effective or productive in that kind of environment, so we overcommunicate to keep it from happening.

That concept applies to your mission and vision too. In his book *Visioneering*, Andy Stanley says you have to share your vision twenty-one times before your team actually hears it and starts to believe in it themselves. Pathfinders must constantly state and restate the company's mission, vision, and core values. You have to learn to tell the story of your business, which is where all those things originate. Talk about the wins and the losses, the good times and the bad—and tell those stories over and over again. If you haven't overcommunicated these things to your team to the point that you're sick and tired of talking about them day after day, week after week, you probably have not communicated well.

What are you really accomplishing when you do this? A lot. You're teaching your team the values system the company is built on. You're showing them they're part of something bigger than themselves. You're inspiring creativity and injecting new energy into how your team approaches their work. You're telling them they are valuable to the mission and that they can win in the future because of how the team has won in the past.

So, where do you deliver all this overcommunication? You have to commit to a regular rhythm of communication opportunities. For us, that starts with our weekly staff meeting. We bring our entire team—more than one thousand people—together every Monday to start off the week just like we did when we had twelve team members. We talk about everything that's going on. We talk about wins, and we talk about our failures. We celebrate milestones and welcome new team members. We do live demonstrations of what teams are working on and what they're learning in the market. And we intentionally set aside time to talk about core values or to revisit our mission and vision.

The one-on-one meetings we talked about in the Role Clarity section are another part of our communication strategy. While one of the goals is to connect with your team about their work, one-on-ones are also about building relationships and trust. Pastor Craig Groeschel says people don't connect with organizations, they connect with people. That's good to remember about your customers and about your team. For you to have a vital, healthy business, you and your leaders need to show you care about more than just what your team members *do*. You need to show you care about who they *are*.

Because good communication goes both ways, we've also developed and use a digital Weekly Reports tool to hear directly from our team members. Like staff meetings, weekly reports are another foundational piece of our culture of communication. Every Friday since the early days of Ramsey, team members have used their weekly reports to share their high and low points of the week, talk about what they worked on and share anything going on in their lives that they want their leaders to know about. The Weekly Reports tool makes it simple for our leaders—even me—to keep a pulse on the team. In less than twenty minutes, I can scan through a thousand weekly reports and get a feel for what's happening across the company and in the lives of our team members.

Of course, as the company has grown, we've added a lot of additional meetings to drive alignment, accountability, and problem-solving. At times, even I think it's overkill, but like I said, overcommunicating is underrated. If we don't communicate well, we're forced to assume—and you know what happens when you *ass*ume!

What Winning Looks Like

As a Pathfinder, it's up to you to get your team aligned on the direction you want the business to go and how you want to get there. And the components we covered in this chapter are essential for accomplishing that. They are what will move you from Pathfinder to the next stage, Trailblazer. As a reminder, here's what we covered:

- Mission statement
- Vision
- Core values
- Role clarity
- Clear communication

These components should feel pretty straightforward now that we've talked about them all, but it's important to remember that once you nail these down, you have an ongoing responsibility to keep them in front of your team. Maybe you're not the chief everything officer anymore, but you are the CRO—chief reminding officer! If you don't get this stuff locked in with your team, your business will plateau. You'll keep bumping up against the same problems over and over again, having to fire people who weren't aligned to the core values, like I had to do, or hiring the wrong people in the first place, which I've also done plenty of times.

On the flip side, you'll know you've graduated from this stage when people start finishing your sentences about the mission, vision, and values of the company. Your team won't be consumers of your culture, they'll be contributors. They'll reinforce the culture themselves by saying things like, "We don't do that (insert toxic behavior) here," to another team member instead of just saying, "I like working here because of the great culture."

Getting this stuff right in the Pathfinder stage will be a tremendous help to your business. You'll have lower turnover and a stronger culture, and your team will have clear lanes of work and responsibility and start making values-based decisions. I'll tell you, as the CEO of Ramsey Solutions, I absolutely love watching all of this happen among our team. It's exciting when your people are bought in to the mission and know what they're doing. Because that's when you finally get to experience the fulfillment that comes from running a business with a true team—warriors who are ready to stand shoulder to shoulder with you to achieve your shared mission. And that's the reward of doing the work to move through the Pathfinder stage.

I know a lot of this stuff might seem obvious to you. You might even think everybody should already know this! The truth is, they don't. And even if they do, at some point they forget. I've been there—you think you have a shared direction because you think you've communicated clearly, but you haven't. You think you have a shared goal, only to find out you don't.

The Pathfinder stage is all about eliminating the distractions and chaos caused by that lack of direction and setting a clear path for your team to follow. You're building a unified team that "gets it"! A team you can trust to deliver the goods and services of your business just like you would—consistently. When you've got that humming along, you're ready for the Trailblazer stage of business.

Scan the QR code below to get a comprehensive step-by-step action plan with tools and resources that will help you get your team pointed in the right direction and making big progress day in and day out.

Client Success Story

Lukas Pirok, **BHMG Engineers, Inc.**

BHMG Engineers, Inc., provides engineering consulting services from its home base in St. Louis, Missouri. When Lukas Pirok became the CEO in 2021, the business was fifty years old—far from a start-up. But in many ways, the company had never pro-gressed past the Pathfinder stage of business, and its culture was in desperate need of an overhaul. The transformation BHMG has undergone in the last few years is a powerful illustration of what happens when leaders take the time to define a mission, vision, and core values for their business that their team can believe in.

When Lukas took the helm of BHMG Engineers, Inc., it was a typical consulting firm with a typical consulting culture. Nobody could tell you what the company's mission, vision, or core values were, but all the team members operated on the same unspoken expectation: *We want you to work more, and we don't care about anything except more productivity.* The natural outcome? The team worked crazy-long hours, and many were away from their families way too often. Lukas immediately set out to change that.

Within weeks of taking on his new role, he laid out his vision for how BHMG would operate going forward. Lukas wanted to make BHMG a company people wanted to work *with* by first making BHMG a company people wanted to work *for.* They would start by tossing out the old outward-facing culture that focused solely on client satisfaction and instead build a culture that cared for its team members. Lukas envisioned hosting team-building events that spouses and kids could come to and leave proud that their husband or wife, mom or dad, worked there.

As Lukas and his leadership team developed new mission and vision statements and core values that would reflect that new direction, they ran into the inevitable question: "Do we have the right people on the bus to champion our new culture?" The truth was, some team members had been with the company a long time, and they were no longer a fit for BHMG's new culture. Lukas and his leadership team made the hard decisions that often come with significant change, doubling down on their new team-centric direction.

Once they had the right people in the right seats, Lukas turned the focus to creating role clarity for each of those seats with Key Results Areas (KRAs).

"It's been a game changer that everyone in the company, from myself to the new engineer, has a KRA," he said. Each leader now owns developing KRAs for their team, making sure each individual team member is bought in to what's expected of them and documenting those KRAs in their HR software. No room for confusion. And given that BHMG is a team of engineers, you can bet those KRAs are detailed and clear. That commitment to clarity is just one more way the company proves how much it cares for its people.

Today, BHMG operates with a culture that lives out its mission statement: **Empowering teams that develop successful relationships for the future.** Their vision, **We see a future where lives are positively affected by family-focused leadership while continually challenging the status quo**, is printed boldly in their café space for anyone—team members and clients—to see.

"In 2021, nobody really knew who we were or what we stood for," Lukas said. "Now, when clients come to our offices, they see those things. They know this is who we are and who we want to be."

Leaders not only took the time to intentionally roll out the mission, vision, and core values out to the team, ensuring buy-in at every level, but they also modeled how to use them in real-time decision-making, all the way up to board-level conversations.

"When we want to make a move, we'll talk about it and push back on it and ask, 'Does this go against a core value?'" Lukas explained.

If the answer is no, they'll charge ahead. But if the answer is yes, the board will pause, dig in, and wrestle through it together until they find the right path forward.

"We want to make sure that the decisions we're making that are best for business still align with our core values over time," Lukas said.

That ruthless commitment to staying true to who they are and where they want to go has been transformative for BHMG. The company's new focus on life balance and flexibility is what team members say they value the most. Their culture is now collaborative, supportive, and engaging—truly a team environment. In an industry where it's hard to retain team members, they haven't had a team member leave in the past eighteen months.

"Now that we're clear on our mission and values, the team is working in the same direction," Lukas said.

It's a completely different place from where the company was a few years ago when Lukas took on the role of CEO, and that momentum is carrying BHMG straight into the Trailblazer stage.

3

TRAILBLAZER

KEY CHALLENGE:

You lack the plan and leaders to scale your business.

WHAT WINNING LOOKS LIKE:

You have a leadership team who is executing
a plan that is scaling your business.

TRAILBLAZER

Hey, Dave, I need to give you a head's up," the email began. "Something happened, and we took care of it, and we did exactly what you would have done. We just wanted you to know we did it because we dropped some money on it."

The email was from my operations guy, one of the three guys who, at that time, was running the company with me. I was on vacation with Sharon and the kids, getting in touch with our Scottish heritage at the Ramsay family's ancestral castle. At this point in the growth of the company, things were starting to get really fun. For the first time ever, I wasn't worried about cash flow. All our numbers—sales, volume, profits—were trending up. We could see the trajectory, a hockey stick up and to the right. It seemed like everything we touched turned to gold, and we were starting to see that we could have a $300 million company someday.

So, when that email came in, I wasn't panicked like I might have been a couple years before, but I was definitely interested to find out what the heck was going on. The email explained that Steve, one of our team members, had a twelve-year-old son, Will, who was at a youth camp in Asheville, North Carolina. Will had been playing dodgeball when he got hit in the head with a ball. Until that moment, no one knew Will had been born with a weak blood vessel in his brain. The impact from the dodgeball caused the aneurysm to burst, and Will was rushed to the hospital. The doctors there phoned Steve and told him that Will had only a few hours to live. Now, there are no commercial flights to Asheville, North Carolina, from Nashville. And it's an eight-hour drive by car. There was no way Steve could get there in time to see his son.

Our HR policy is the Golden Rule, straight out of the book of Matthew: "Do to others what you would have them do to you" (7:12 NIV). If it's good enough for Jesus, it's good enough for me and my team. So, when they heard about Will, my team did what we always do: Treat others the way we want to be treated. How would I want someone to treat me if my kid had a few hours to live and he's an eight-hour drive away? Well, I know what our team did. They chartered a jet for Steve for eight thousand bucks, and he was at his son's side in less than two hours.

I felt a lot of things as I read that email. Mainly, I felt heartbreak for Steve and his family over what they were going through. What we didn't know at the time was that Will would survive the aneurysm and eventually come home! He had a tough road ahead of him to recover from the damage that was done, though. So Steve organized the WillPower 5K race to help raise money and awareness for the condition that led to Will's injury. And this time, the entire company jumped in to support Steve and his family. That tradition continued for several years, even after Steve left the company. And the great news is that today, Will is a grown young man and doing well, thank God.

I think you'll understand when I tell you how proud I was of my leadership team for the way they took care of Steve. They never asked me what to do because they *knew*, without a doubt, that I would handle it exactly the way they did. At that moment, as I sat at a dinner table in a Scottish castle, I realized we'd hit a whole new level. I didn't have to carry the whole company all by myself anymore. That moment showed me that all the work we'd done in the Pathfinder stage to define our mission and vision, develop our core values, and communicate them—over and over again—was starting to work. The alignment we'd created meant I could stop being hyperfocused on the day to day, and I could start thinking about how to become that $300 million business I knew was possible.

Hitting the Ceiling

Now, before you get the wrong idea and assume everything was perfect, let me be clear: We still had a lot of work to do to have a shot at fulfilling our potential as a business and have the kind of impact I believed we were capable of. While my leadership team and I had clearly built a ton of trust, there were still too few people trying to hold the business together. In fact, the biggest challenges business owners face during the Trailblazer stage is that you don't have the leadership team or the strategic plan you need to scale your business.

I had three guys leading the company with me, but the team and the business were growing so fast that the four of us became a huge bottleneck. We didn't have the capacity to support the amount of work we wanted to do. On top of that, we weren't planning far enough out to assign resources where they were needed most. Our business unit leaders were playing tug-of-war over people and processes in an effort to get their work done.

Another common challenge Trailblazers deal with that we had to overcome was the fact that while our business had exploded, our processes hadn't changed much from the early days. We were still entering every customer's bank and debit card info by hand, for crying out loud! Did it work? Sure. But in addition to the enormous security risk, it was a lot of extra work, and working harder just wasn't getting it done. We had to figure out how to work smarter. When your processes are not strong enough to support your big vision, it's like trying to put out a fire using a bucket that's full of holes. You'll never get enough water in that bucket as long as it keeps leaking out.

SIGNS YOU MAY BE IN THE
TRAILBLAZER STAGE

Working longer hours isn't working like it did before.

Hiring more people to solve problems doesn't work anymore.

Processes and systems are not strong enough to support the vision.

You're striving to establish plans and processes to scale your business.

You're working on the basics of a powerful and healthy organization to get reliable results.

FRUSTRATIONS YOU FACE IN THE
TRAILBLAZER STAGE

You're trying to figure out how to operationalize the company.

You don't know how to get your leaders to think about bigger-picture problems.

You're having trouble scaling the business.

You feel stretched way too thin.

The team has more work than they can handle.

Business owners who are in the Trailblazer stage often say things like:

"I feel like we're flying by the seat of our pants. It makes me sick to my stomach."

"It's hard to get everyone in the same room, and we really need to so that we know everyone gets the same message."

"As the owner, I struggle with leading leaders. I don't want to manage people or projects directly myself. But I want my leadership team to be visionary leaders, and I'm not sure how to help them do that."

"I want my leaders to learn in five years what took me ten years to learn. How do I help them avoid making all the mistakes I made?"

These problems feel big, especially when your biggest problem used to be how to make payroll by Friday. But the Trailblazer stage is full of opportunity too. Like us, a lot of owners in this stage see, maybe for the first time, that it's possible to grow the business tenfold given the right circumstances. I'll show you how we addressed these challenges at Ramsey Solutions—sometimes against my better judgment—as we worked through the Trailblazer stage.

Fulfilling Your Business's Potential

Jeff Bezos has an interesting team-building principle he calls the two-pizza rule. The idea is to keep your team size small—small enough to feed with two pizzas. Why? The smaller the team, the better the communication and collaboration. It's just easier to keep a smaller team on the same page.

In the Pathfinder stage of business, your team likely fit the two-pizza rule, and you could personally share the mission, vision, and values to create the alignment your team needed to be successful. But as a Trailblazer, your team has probably become too large to feed with two pizzas, and that means you can no longer rely on one-off conversations to keep everybody plugged in. Now's the time to start the process of hardwiring those foundational pieces of your company culture into your operations. Your hiring process, comp strategy, communications rhythms, and everything else you do need to stem from your mission, vision, and values to keep your team and your company unified and moving in the right direction as you grow.

That begins, of course, with your leadership team. You need people at the top who can finish your sentences and make decisions just like you would even when you aren't in the room. The goal is to build a level of leaders who are so aligned with your mission, vision, and values that you can delegate to them without hesitation—and this goes way beyond delegating tasks. The Trailblazer has to begin delegating actual leadership of teams or areas of the business. You need rock stars leading things like all of marketing, all of operations, all of finance, all of HR. The first time I felt like we actually had a shot at fulfilling our potential was when I added our first CFO and head of HR to the leadership team.

With a group of leaders like that working alongside you at an executive level, you're ready for the next huge step you'll take as a Trailblazer: strategic planning. This is where you look ahead to identify what the company will look like in the next three, five or ten years so you can get your team working on the right things to bring that vision to life. Those two things—the right leaders and the right plan—have the potential to blow your business wide open!

In addition to operationalizing your culture, building a solid leadership team, and landing a sound strategic plan, you've also got to identify and implement processes you can rely on. Up to a point, personal heroics, like working late and working on the weekends, are enough to get stuff done. But eventually that breaks down. There literally aren't enough hours in the day to keep up. To scale your business, you need processes that generate repeatable results and don't require you to hire more and more people to manage them. All those things boil down to the four key skills we'll talk about in this chapter that will move you from Trailblazer to Peak Performer:

- Intentional culture
- Leadership development
- Strategic planning
- Repeatable processes

INTENTIONAL CULTURE

In the Pathfinder stage, getting clear on your mission, vision, and values helps you create direction for your company and your team. They are the foundation of your company's culture, and you need them to conquer that stage of business. But by themselves, they don't *create* a company culture. That happens in the Trailblazer stage, when you begin to hardwire your mission, vision, and values into all the processes in your business. When your mission, vision, and values define how you do business—how you hire people, how you pay people, how and why you fire people, how you communicate and celebrate team members, and even how you do meetings— you bring your company culture to life for your team.

As I mentioned before, it's not possible for you to do this on your own. There aren't enough hours in the day for you to have all the individual conversations it takes to operationalize the company culture for a growing team. This was a tough realization for me because it forced me to the conclusion that it was past time for me to hire an HR director. I avoided that hire because at the time, I didn't have a real appreciation for HR. Honestly, I thought of HR as a bunch of bean counters who would try to tell me who to hire and how to run my business—like a bunch of lawyers. To me, HR was the place employees went to whine instead of working out their issues with their leader. I had no idea how important a well-staffed and great-functioning HR team would be for the growth of the business.

When we did make that hire, though, we hit the jackpot with Rick Perry. Rick was a genius not only because he didn't do any of the dumb things I had worried HR would do, but also because, in the nearly twenty years he was with Ramsey, he changed the whole shape of the company—in a good way. In the Pathfinder chapter, I told you about how Rick helped us recognize and document our core values. That was our first step toward operationalizing our culture because it made it possible to scale the way we taught our leaders and team members the principles that guide all our business and personnel decisions. We also started using the core values as the basis of our hiring process so that, in addition to finding qualified thoroughbreds who could do the work, we also were able to increase the odds of hiring people who would be a good culture fit. It was brilliant! (And I wish we'd done it much earlier.)

So, why is this important? Why put so much time and energy into building and operationalizing a quality culture? In *EntreLeadership*, I wrote about the five enemies of unity:

Poor Communication

A team *must* be on the same page. If the right hand doesn't know what the left hand is doing, disunity, anger, and frustration will fill your company.

Lack of Shared Purpose

A lack of a shared purpose causes a lack of unity. If the team doesn't share the goals of leadership and of each other, there isn't unity.

Gossip

I absolutely hate gossip. If people have an issue, they need to speak up to their leader, not out to their teammates who can't fix it.

Unresolved Disagreements

Disagreements that go unresolved grow. They eventually paralyze people. Leaders must step in to help resolve the problem.

Sanctioned Incompetence

When a team member is incompetent, for any reason, and leadership won't act, the good team members become demoralized.

Any of these issues has the power to wreck your company overnight. But a strong, intentional culture that defines the way your business works creates unity within your team. It is the infrastructure that defends your company against the enemies of unity. But a strong culture doesn't spontaneously appear. Peter Drucker, author and famed management consultant, nailed this idea on the head: "Only three things happen naturally in organizations: friction, confusion, and under-performance. Everything else requires leadership." That's why the Trailblazer must "make every effort to keep the unity of the Spirit through the bond of peace" (Ephesians 4:3 NIV). And that begins by first defining your mission, vision, and core values as a Pathfinder and then, as a Trailblazer, making them concrete for your team members by building them into the processes they use every day.

LEADERSHIP DEVELOPMENT

When you delegate a task to another leader, you're telling the leader to get that task done. But when you delegate leading to leaders, you're not just delegating tasks. You're delegating the careers and lives of the people on that person's team. If you're like me, you probably have a lot of feelings about turning over that kind of responsibility. How will that person treat or mistreat their team in my name? How could that affect the company's reputation? Will the team be taken care of? Will the leaders get the work done? Are they enabling bad behavior? Is everyone goofing off?

I'll be honest, you will probably run into some problems as you build up your leadership team. I had one leader who loved to celebrate wins with his team by treating them to pizza or ice cream when they hit their numbers. One day, he came to my office to invite me to join in that month's ice cream celebration, but the team hadn't hit their numbers. Now, I don't have a problem with ice cream. I don't have a problem with the team celebrating when they hit their numbers. I *do* have a problem celebrating when the team *hasn't* hit their numbers.

That's what can happen when you delegate to delegate to delegate. It's like playing a game of telephone. Your original message is "Celebrate the wins!" But by the time it gets to all your leaders, it's just "Celebrate!" As a Trailblazer, you'll have to teach each layer of leadership how things work. In fact, a big part of your job in the Trailblazer stage will be to bring what Jim Collins, in his book *Good to Great*, calls the last 10 percent of truth. You'll be the one who stands up and says, "This is not okay," "We're headed in the wrong direction," and, "We have to fix this." Just like I had to do that day when I made it clear that it's okay to celebrate as long as we're celebrating the right things.

I mentioned before that back in the early days of the business, I had three guys running things with me. It was the first time we had layers of leadership that were effective. I had a ton of confidence in them because number one, they showed me in the way they handled the issue with Steve and his son that they understood how to lead the way I needed them to. And number two, they were making tons of progress in their areas and getting a tremendous amount of work done with their teams. But we had big issues to fix. Anything the company did had to come through the four of us, creating a leadership bottleneck. Plus, each area was built as a separate profit center, creating silos that kept us from thinking strategically across the whole business. Winning in our business became a game of getting your pet project approved by one of the four of us. VPs started vying for our time ruthlessly. We called it "VP on VP violence," and it became kind of an inside joke with the team. We even made a short parody video about it for our team Christmas party. But the constraint it put on our business was no joke.

We've restructured the company several times since those days, working through multiple iterations of executive-level leadership. Today at Ramsey Solutions, our top leadership team is our operating board. Every Monday, after our staff meeting, the operating board meets to hash out what needs to happen for the business to win. These are all leaders who have a ton of experience. Most of them have been with the company for over a decade. A few are newer but had a lot of experience before they joined the team. They are what we refer to as Leaders of Leaders and have been winning in their leadership roles for years.

As a Trailblazer, your leadership team won't necessarily need the same level of business or leadership experience Ramsey currently has on its operating board. At this stage, your focus is on building a strong cross-functional leadership team that can handle the challenges that come with rapid growth so you can seize the opportunity that exists in the market. The good news is that the people who have the potential to help you 10x your business are also the ones who have the potential to grow into executive leaders. Here's what I look for:

- Ability to spot and develop talent in key roles
- Ability to grow not just a great team but great leaders
- Ability to cast vision and inspire teams
- Ability to think and plan strategically

As you observe leaders within your team, look for these traits. These are the folks you can lean on to build your leadership team and help you move your business into the Peak Performer stage.

Since we're just scratching the surface here on the topic of leadership development, we'll give you access to a couple more important resources at the end of this chapter, including The EntreLeadership Reading Guide. Whole books have been written on how to build strong and effective leadership teams, and since leaders are readers, I strongly suggest you make reading a habit. I've become a student of the work of experts like Dr. Henry Cloud, Patrick Lencioni, Jim Collins, John Maxwell, and others who've become friends of the company and speak at EntreLeadership Summit, one of our annual leadership events.

You'll also get access to a seven-step guide to help you build an intentional leadership development plan for your business using principles we follow at Ramsey.

STRATEGIC PLANNING

One day, several years back, I happened to see a large group of our *Financial Peace University* team heading into our conference center. Of course, I was curious about why so many people weren't working and bringing in the revenue they were hired to bring in. When I asked one of the leaders what was going on, she informed me that the team was participating in a two-day strat-op. She might as well have been speaking a foreign language. What the heck is a strat-op? Turns out, the goal of a strat-op is strategic operations planning. Essentially, the team was going to spend two days' worth of payroll sitting around tables and talking about a five-year plan for the business. On top of all that, they'd paid someone—someone who didn't run a company—several thousand dollars to facilitate the meeting and tell *us* how to run a company.

The whole thing went against the grain with me in so many ways. I'm an entrepreneur. I believe in killing things and dragging them back to the cave. Up to that point, our business strategy was to do that enough times to make it to Friday. And if we did that enough times to make it to December, our strategy worked. The idea that so many people would take time away from the work that would bring in revenue today to talk about dreams and ideas for tomorrow was lost on me.

I have a bunch of folks on my team who have their master's degree in business administration, and I have them to thank for introducing me to the concept of strategic planning. I have a degree in DUMB, not an MBA. But what I've learned about folks with an MBA is that they understand the value of getting a thirty-thousand-foot view of your business so you can steer around problems instead of barreling right into them. That's really what the team wanted to accomplish in their strategic planning sessions.

Much to my surprise, that first planning session actually worked! The team went back to work energized by the plans they made, and that profit center immediately went gangbusters! After that, we started doing strategic planning on a regular basis company-wide. And once I realized strategic planning will help you solve growth challenges that can't be overcome by hiring more people (our usual go-to problem-solving method), I started to buy in to the idea too. If your business is experiencing any of these issues, it's time to get more strategic with your planning:

- Your revenue has plateaued.
- Your market has changed.
- Your business is experiencing a crisis.
- You're making decisions in silos.

Do I enjoy going to these strategic planning sessions now? No—they're about as enjoyable as a root canal for me. But my son, Daniel, who is now the president of Ramsey Solutions, is wonderful at strategic planning. And I do love what happens when we as a leadership team align on our plan. We lay out a vision for it, put stories around it, and create dashboards so we can see the work we need to do and track our progress.

Don't miss that last part. Strategic planning isn't finished until you document your plan and define how you're going to track your progress. At Ramsey, our leadership teams leave planning sessions with a Desired Future Dashboard for their area of the business. It captures the plan we've all aligned to and boils it down to three elements that we can roll out to the team: a desired future statement that paints a picture of where we want the business to be in the next twelve months, the defining objectives that describe the chunks of work we need to do to get there, and the key results that define which metrics we're going to use to measure success.

Each of these components are essential for knowing where you're headed and what winning looks like for your company. Think of your desired future as the destination, your defining objectives as your road map, and your key results as the milestones that confirm you're on track to get where you want to go. Once it's all laid out, your leaders should consistently check in on the Desired Future

Dashboard and use a simple system to track progress on your defining objectives and key results. We use color codes: green for on track, yellow for slightly off pace, and red for falling behind. Pretty straightforward. But this helps us surface problems quickly so we can have the right discussions (or debates) to get us back on track.

Now, once you've carved out the time and committed to doing the strategic planning work, here's how you can get your team started on creating and maintaining a Desired Future Dashboard:

Step 1: Brainstorm

Gather your key leaders and decision-makers in a strategic planning meeting and ask, "Where do we want our business to go in the next twelve months?"

Step 2: Narrow the Options

Focus on narrowing your options to three to five ideas that will define your strategy for the next year.

Step 3: Create Your Desired Future Statement

This should be a simple yet powerful statement that clearly communicates your goals to your team. A useful formula to follow is: "By [DATE], we will [CREATE OR DO THIS], resulting in [THIS]."

Step 4: Define Your Objectives

These are four to six challenges that must be overcome to achieve the desired future. Your objectives answer the question "What must be true to reach our desired future?" They're the foundational steps toward achieving your desired future.

Step 5: Assign Ownership

Each objective needs an owner. This person will define specific key results, ensure the team stays focused on the right work, and report regularly on the team's status.

Step 6: Track Your Progress

Set aside times in weekly leadership meetings to review your Desired Future Dashboard and discuss whether objectives and key results are on track or if anything needs to change. Check out the example below to see what this looks like in action.

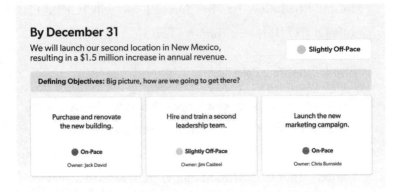

Source: EntreLeadership Elite Desired Future Tool

The best thing about strategic planning and tools like the Desired Future Dashboard is that they get us where we want to go much faster than we would without it. It's too easy for entrepreneurs like you and me to get distracted by a shiny new idea instead of focusing on the high-return activities we already have in place. On top of that, it can be tough for entrepreneurial types to give up on ideas that just aren't working out. Strategic planning helps you develop the discipline to choose the best things over the good things and avoid distractions so you keep moving toward the truly important goals you set.

Like I said, these aren't my favorite meetings to sit through, and they may not be for you either. But if there's anything worse than attending a strategic planning session, it's attending one that doesn't accomplish anything. At the end of this chapter, you'll get access to two resources to help you do this right: our guide to planning and running a strategic planning session that will lead to meaningful insights you can act on to push your business forward and a more in-depth look at the process for developing a Desired Future Dashboard to track your progress on that plan.

REPEATABLE PROCESSES

In the same way I waited too long to hire Ramsey's first HR director, I also ended up hiring our first CFO several million dollars in revenue too late. That's because I'm a hardwired sales guy. An entrepreneur's entrepreneur. No matter what, I'm getting the deal done because that's the only way to make sure we live to fight another day. The upside of being wired that way is that we did live to fight another day, and now we have a business that's helped millions of people change their lives for the better. The downside is that I didn't always have a lot of appreciation for people who didn't follow that same approach.

Bookkeeping and accounting—and the people who live for that stuff—fall into that category of folks whose strengths are completely different from mine. I do love being in the numbers because I'm a math nerd, but I loathe the accounting process. That's why one of the first three people I hired was somebody to do bookkeeping so I wouldn't have to. That was a good decision while we were a smaller business. But a few years later, I looked up and realized I was running a $14 million business with just a bookkeeper, and that was just dumb! Once we added a CFO to our leadership team, though, it was easy to see what we'd been missing. And it was great because he saw things that helped us. He started moving stuff around and creating metrics, and I was like, "Okay, that's cool." He developed systems and made us more sophisticated, which allowed us to get to another level.

Hiring an HR director and a CFO helped move Ramsey Solutions to the next level. Now, I'm not saying that not having those roles is what's wrong with your company. But you may be missing a layer of leadership and an area of sophistication that could be keeping you from scaling. And you thought it was just that you needed to sell more. Because that's what I thought. I always thought I could outsell my stupidity. I'm still trying at times.

What Winning Looks Like

If there is an overarching theme for the Trailblazer stage, it's the idea of scaling—scaling your leadership, scaling your planning, and scaling your processes so you can scale your business. As a Treadmill Operator, you planted the seeds of sound business principles like time management, delegation, and budgeting. As a Pathfinder, you created alignment for your team by defining your mission and vision and establishing core values. As a Trailblazer, that work begins to bear fruit, like it did when my team showed me they not only understood *how* to make the decisions I would make, but they also understood *why* I would make those decisions.

This is a pivotal moment for your business. I'll use an example from what I teach about building wealth to show you what I mean. Wealth building begins with a strong foundation for your money, meaning you've got to get out and stay out of debt and save up an emergency fund. That alone will create more financial security than most people have ever experienced in their lives, and they could decide to stop right there and simply enjoy that level of security. But to build the kind of wealth that changes family trees, you have to keep building on that foundation. You have to invest and pay off your home. You have to keep pushing and working toward the future you envision. The same is true in the Trailblazer stage for your business. As a reminder, here's what we covered:

- Intentional culture
- Leadership development
- Strategic planning
- Repeatable processes

If you've come this far, there's a potential in the market for your business to grow exponentially. But unless you keep pushing and building on the foundation you've already built, it just won't happen. Your leadership team must take more ownership. Your business strategy must become more sophisticated. Your company culture has to become operational. Your processes must scale to meet the needs of the business. In short, it's time to work smarter, not just harder, and you as the Trailblazer are still the driving force making all that happen.

Scan the QR code below to get a comprehensive step-by-step action plan with tools and resources that will help you scale your business so it can have the impact that matches its potential.

Client Success Story

Katie Clapp, A&C Plastics, Inc.

Katie Clapp is the president of A&C Plastics, Inc., in Houston, Texas. They're an incredible example of a company in the Trailblazer stage of business. Their plethora of plastic products are sold to a variety of manufacturing companies and are used in making retail signs, shower doors, skylights, space suits, and even pianos. Some of the company's bulletproof materials are used for drive-through bank windows, convenience stores, and prison windows. Not to mention their acrylic sheet material that was in very high demand with the pandemic crisis in 2020.

When Polycast Corp. (a plastic sheet distributor) decided to shut down their Houston warehouse in 1973, Carolyn and Myrl Faulk saw an opportunity.

"Polycast didn't think they were making enough money in Houston, but what was 'no money' to them was big money to us," Carolyn explained. "We took the $5,000 we had saved and started up the business with a client list and no inventory." That was the humble beginning of what would become A&C Plastics, Inc.

In the mid-1980s, Carolyn bought out Myrl's half of the business in their divorce. She was a woman business leader at a time and in an industry that wasn't woman friendly. She was figuring things out on the fly. And as she built a thriving business, Carolyn passed her knowledge and example on to her daughter, Katie.

And she did a pretty effective job. Katie grew up spending summers working in the business. One of her earliest memories was having to lick and seal hundreds of envelopes for customer mailers—which earned her a whopping $1 per hour. Katie is now the president of A&C.

In 1998, Katie joined the team as a part-time receptionist. Back then, the company had about twenty team members and didn't have a lot of technology. So Katie started implementing a variety of technologies to help improve the ways the company interacted with clients. Then she spent time working with the marketing and accounting departments, where she helped bring new efficiencies. By the time she stepped into the president role, Katie had worked in every area and department of A&C.

Under this mother-daughter team, A&C has seen tremendous growth. But it's taken a lot of intentionality to put the right pieces in place to scale the right way. In 2012, after uncovering an internal embezzlement scheme (that cost the company about $2 million), Katie knew she needed help learning how to effectively run their business.

"I just felt completely lost after the embezzlement took place," she admitted. That's when Katie and Carolyn attended a one-day EntreLeadership business event in Austin, Texas. The learnings they took away from that event led to their attending EntreLeadership Master Series events, where Katie learned tactical tools to help guide and grow their business as well as how to pour into her leaders.

With each event, Carolyn and Katie started implementing the things they were learning. They started off in 2013 by developing a mission statement, a vision statement, and identifying the core values for A&C. That was a huge step since they'd never done that in the past—and it provided a foundational framework for the company to move forward.

Katie worked with their HR department to help communicate company culture and core values to new team members during their revamped onboarding process. She still vividly remembers witnessing one of her leaders clearly explain the company core values to a new team member—and how relieved she felt that one of her leaders was communicating the same things she would have communicated.

Today, everyone knows and can recite the company core values easily.

She also took a step back and evaluated their hiring process. Katie realized that, for too long, they were just hiring anyone who applied for a job. That resulted in a bunch of the wrong people being on the team and in the wrong seats. Yikes! Now, they've implemented a six-step process to bring in the right people for the right positions.

All that foundational work paid off when 2020 suddenly transformed the world into what seemed like a maze of plexiglass barriers. Being a provider of acrylic sheets, A&C saw their business double. Prior to 2020, the company had fifty-five team members—today, they have over 105.

Since the company was large enough during the pandemic and they were able to supply acrylic sheets to so many different clients, they attracted a lot of new customers. Many of those new customers ended up staying with A&C for their ongoing signage needs—especially since so many smaller plastic companies shut down because of the pandemic. It was a pivotal time for their business.

While A&C experienced fantastic growth in their business, sales, and profits in the post-2020 world, all that growth revealed some gaps—specifically, they were missing a fully functional leadership team. As the company literally doubled almost overnight, Katie had to move people into leadership roles whether or not they had any leadership experience. As a result, they lost some key people and valued team members.

These days, Katie is focused on developing her leaders as well as creating a Desired Future Dashboard. After an internal strategic planning workshop, they've put together one-year, three-year, and five-year plans for the business. Katie's leadership team meets twice a month to look at their strategic plan and track how well they're doing in working toward their goals. Now, Katie and her team are equipped to move in the same direction.

"After updating our systems, streamlining our processes, and building a strong leadership team, we're now able to scale the business and move into Peak Performer."

STAGE

4

PEAK PERFORMER

KEY CHALLENGE:

Your business has become too comfortable.

WHAT WINNING LOOKS LIKE:

You and your team have a relentless culture of getting better.

STAGE

4

PEAK PERFORMER

In 2003, my book *The Total Money Makeover* was published, and it was an instant bestseller. By 2005, it had sold almost two million copies. One of the interesting things that happens when you have a huge bestseller like that is the media reaction. Everyone wants to talk to you. Back then, I did all the media interviews, and every show you can imagine called and invited me to talk about the book. It was amazing! There was one day when I was on Larry King, Sally Jessy Raphael, and Gayle King (one of Oprah's friends)—all in the same day. I was on the *Today* show, *Good Morning America*, and Fox for the first time during this season as well.

The only other show we wanted to be on was *The Oprah Winfrey Show*. In those days, if you were on Oprah's show and she said people needed to read your book, you'd sell a million copies overnight. So I kept pushing to get us on Oprah. We sent the show producers recordings, the book, and all kinds of stuff to get their attention. Every so often, we'd hear from one of her six production teams, and we would instantly—a little too eagerly—respond, "Yes! What do you want us to do?" Then . . . radio silence. We wouldn't hear back from them. We did this same song and dance with them so many times that it became a running joke at the office that we had *almost* been on Oprah more than anybody. It's funny now, but it sure wasn't then.

During this time, Lesley Stahl from *60 Minutes* called and said she wanted to do a feature on *60 Minutes* with me. I had a lot of mixed feelings about that. On the one hand, it was a huge opportunity to reach people who'd never heard of us. But I'd seen a lot of *60 Minutes* pieces that got into negative stuff, and we knew it was possible that they might try to misrepresent our mission, and that could hurt our momentum. But one of our core values is that we don't make decisions based on fear. So even though we were excited *and* scared, we agreed to do the piece.

Working with the *60 Minutes* team was kind of crazy—but a lot of fun too. They followed me to film a six-thousand-person event we held in Louisville, Kentucky, and while we were in town preparing for the event, the Louisville Minor League Baseball team (the Bats) invited me to throw out the first pitch at one of their games. Now, I don't play baseball, so I knew if I attempted this, it would be super embarrassing. But the baseball team's event planners and the *60 Minutes* crew wore me down until I agreed to do it.

So, there I was on the ball field, convinced I was about to screw up this pitch and convinced they'd use it to humiliate me on *60 Minutes*. They even had a mic on me to capture every embarrassing detail. I was standing on the mound, freaking out when the team mascot—a giant, winged bat— came flapping out to help me. Seriously. I had never met the guy before, but he saw the camera there and was really hamming it up. Then he leaned over to me and happened to speak almost directly into the microphone, "Hey, Dave, this is my extra job to get out of debt." The producer from *60 Minutes* accused me—jokingly—of setting the whole thing up. Are you kidding me? Who would think of getting the personal testimony of a giant bat? I didn't—but it was absolutely perfect.

While we waited for the *60 Minutes* piece to air, you could feel the nervous tension building as we all wondered how the piece would come across. Finally, it aired, and when the segment ended, I was completely blown away! It was all positive—twelve minutes and 100 percent of it was a positive reflection of Ramsey Solutions. On *60 Minutes*! When you look that up in the Bible, it's called a miracle.

It turns out that Oprah's people were watching *60 Minutes* too. They called us up the next week, and this time, they meant it. A small group of us went up to tape the show with Oprah, but it didn't go exactly how we'd planned. Oprah disagreed with me about the best advice for a couple we interviewed on the show. And I argued with her about it because she was wrong. So she never mentioned anything about *The Total Money Makeover*, and all we got out of it was some really good footage of me arguing with Oprah.

Still, it was Oprah—the most popular and influential talk show at that time. It was great exposure. So when Oprah's team told us the show would run in April, we called all the bookstores so they could have plenty of copies of *The Total Money Makeover* on hand to handle the Oprah onslaught. Then Oprah's team called back and said they wouldn't run the show until September. The bookstores weren't happy about it, and neither were we.

Then *60 Minutes* called us again. They had run our segment the previous November, and it was one of their highest-rated shows. They were planning to air it again during the network's reruns the last week of August. We were about to get another hit with *60 Minutes* followed two weeks later by our Oprah hit.

After all the ups and downs and starts and stops with Oprah's team, we were about to get more (mostly) positive media attention than money could buy! Things were lining up better than we could have planned, and we were riding a wave of unbelievable momentum—which is, of course, a good thing for any business. But there were some yellow flags signaling trouble. The team started to show signs of an attitude shift. When momentum is on your side, it can make you look like you're better than you are. It's easier to believe "We got this!" or "Success is easy!" or "God is blessing us!" Even worse is the idea that you simply got lucky, or that God is sending lightning so you can simply stand back and watch.

We had to figure out a way to recognize the positive side of the momentum we were experiencing without falling into a trap of complacency. We couldn't let the team forget the hard work and hard times that, combined with God's blessings, were the real reasons why we were winning. And if we wanted to keep on winning, we couldn't let up!

Know Your Enemy

The Peak Performer stage is incredibly awesome. Your business and your team are firing on all cylinders. You're setting the standard in your part of the world and setting the pace in your industry. All the work you and your team put in to get to this stage is paying off. You're helping a ton of people and generating a lot of value for everyone involved, including you and your family. You get to bring in team members who are smarter than you about certain things—smarter even than the whole team. And they can move the entire team with their knowledge base.

Do you know how long it's been since I have had to do something that I suck at or that I hate? As a Peak Performer, you have the team and the means to delegate those things. I don't even remember the last time I snapped a projector screen together or set up chairs like I did back in our Treadmill Operator stage. You've built a ton of momentum by scaling your systems and investing time into your strategic planning. You have clarity, and everything's a blast. You've worked like crazy for a long time to get to this point, and if your business hangs out in this stage for the next couple of decades, that's not a bad thing. You're winning big time!

All that winning and momentum also make it incredibly tempting to take your foot off the gas and coast for a while. I admit, I became less attentive to the little things. I had the luxury of delegating to thoroughbred leaders, so I knew that everything was covered. But that meant it took me a while to realize I wasn't digging in as deep as I had during the earlier stages of our business. I was far from checked out, but I was taking a few more vacations, relying on others a bit more than I should have, and not asking as many hard questions of people I had come to trust.

That's what we call complacency, and it's the Peak Performer's true enemy. You can and should take pride in the fact that your business is doing great, and at the same time, you need to guard yourself, the team, and the culture against becoming too comfortable. In the same way you might take your eye off the ball, your team can forget to be scrappy like they were in the old days. If you let that go for too long, the team starts to get soft, and their resourcefulness and creative problem-solving muscles start to atrophy. Next, you'll start to see bureaucracy pop up, and the last thing any business needs is a bunch of corporate busybodies draining the team of their entrepreneurial zeal. The Peak Performer has to drive home the fact, to themselves and to the team, that you're not done yet. Nothing, including your business, can maintain peak performance on its own. You have to keep pouring your energy into it for it to remain excellent.

SIGNS YOU MAY BE IN THE
PEAK PERFORMER STAGE

Your team has the feeling of "We're doing great."

You feel the need to guard the culture and protect team unity.

You're trying to identify what's next.

FRUSTRATIONS YOU FACE IN THE
PEAK PERFORMER STAGE

You wonder if your team even needs you anymore.

You're having trouble identifying what your role is at this point.

You feel as if the team is afraid to take any risks.

You're starting to recognize that leadership has grown too comfortable.

How to Fight Complacency

In his book *How the Mighty Fall: And Why Some Companies Never Give In*, Jim Collins says, "I've come to see institutional decline like a staged disease: harder to detect but easier to cure in the early stages, easier to detect but harder to cure in the later stages. An institution can look strong on the outside but already be sick on the inside." We've taken that to heart at Ramsey Solutions, so we've employed a specific strategy to fight institutional decline (aka complacency): building a culture of relentless improvement. What does that look like? Well, we will never be too big or too sophisticated to be scrappy about how we get work done. Our scrappiness, our willingness to do whatever it takes to produce excellent work, is what got us here, so we'll always keep that scrappy spirit. At the end of the day, every line of code and every book shipped out of Ramsey Solutions is for the people outside our walls. We can't ever lose sight of that. We refuse to coast. Instead, we're going to lean in and be world class in everything we do because that's how we will continue to impact lives.

Where does that kind of attitude start? At the top, of course. Peter Drucker says, "Your first and foremost job as a leader is to take charge of your own energy and then help to orchestrate the energy of those around you." It's so true. If complacency is the enemy, then focusing on constant improvement at every level of the business is the weapon. In this chapter, we'll cover the four most important actions the Peak Performer can take to build that culture of relentless improvement:

- Recommit to your mission
- Inspire your team
- Reflect and respond
- Proactive disruption

RECOMMIT TO YOUR MISSION

We've spent a lot of time talking about how to get your team aligned, bought in, and working toward your company's mission. A little later in this chapter, we'll talk about how to inspire your team in the Peak Performer stage, but first, I want to talk about how important it is to make sure you're stoking your own fire. This is usually pretty easy to do when you've gone into business because you've got something inside you that drives you to serve people and make a difference. If you're in business just to get rich, then it's easy for you to wander, but that's not most EntreLeaders.

I'm in a unique situation in that I spend hours every day talking to my customers on our radio show and podcasts. I not only get to hear about how they're struggling, about the horrible money advice they've gotten, and about how money mistakes are destroying their relationships, but I also get to hear from people who have turned all that around—sometimes against impossible odds. They come onto our show, share their incredible stories of life-change, and scream, "I'M DEBT-FREE!" And I still get chills every time. The single mom who clawed her way out of debt, the young couple who took on three jobs, the widow who is debt-free for the first time in her life—they've all changed their lives and the lives of their families forever.

And even after decades of hearing those stories, I still get choked up. Our team does too. I can look through the studio glass every day we're recording *The Ramsey Show* and spot team members tearing up at those Debt-Free Screams just like I do. Many of our folks even get face-to-face time with our customers, either while volunteering at our events or calling them up to talk with them about their experiences with our products. Our team members know who's on the other side of all their work, and that keeps them on fire for what we're working toward. It drives home a message we have written on a sign outside our team member entrance: "Someone's life will change because you came to work today."

Now, I'm pretty sure I know what you're thinking. All these emotional stories and life-changing moments make it easy for me and the team to stay plugged in to the mission. But I'll challenge you that if you slow down long enough, you'll see moments like these in your business too. If you've got an HVAC business, I guarantee you that if it's 95 degrees outside and somebody's air goes out, it's emotional when it gets fixed! Your business saved the day, maybe saved dinner, and definitely saved a married couple from an argument.

As a Peak Performer, your business is successful, and that's evidence of the lives you've impacted and the people you've served. You simply cannot take that success and that impact for granted. If you allow yourself and your team to dial back your intensity, your success and impact will also diminish. That's why you can't settle for less than excellence and relentless improvement, even now when your business is running like a well-oiled machine.

INSPIRE YOUR TEAM

Back at the beginning of this chapter, I mentioned that momentum, when it's on your side, has a way of making you look better than you are. From the outside, people see your momentum and often make the mistake of thinking of you as an "overnight success." From the inside, you and your team can misinterpret your momentum as a sign that "you've arrived" and your days of hustle and scrappiness are behind you. When I saw that happening with my team, I decided we needed to find a way to quantify momentum so we could all have a better understanding of how it really works. A few of my longtime team members and I started looking back over the actions and events that had propelled us forward—all the mountain-top highs and ocean-bottom lows—and eventually we landed on a theorem. It's a mathematical formula of sorts—not so much about numbers but principles. I call it the Momentum Theorem: Focused intensity over time, multiplied by God, equals unstoppable momentum. It blows the idea of "overnight success" and "we have arrived" out of the water.

THE
MOMENTUM
THEOREM

$$\frac{Fi}{T}(G)=M$$

Today, the Momentum Theorem is one of our core values. We even had special Momentum Theorem coins made, and every team member gets one when they hit their one-year anniversary (team members call it their Ramseyversary). It's one small way we remind our team that for our company to maintain its momentum, they have to live up to their end of the Momentum Theorem bargain by bringing their effort and their focus, consistently, day after day.

If you want to hear more about the Momentum Theorem and how it can help you grow your business, you're in luck. At the end of this chapter, you'll get access to *The Momentum Theorem*—a Quick Read I wrote to unpack the entire concept.

We also understand that maintaining focus is hard. As a Peak Performer, you have to keep rallying the troops, and the best way we've found to do that is through the stories of the company's struggles and successes. It's easy to feel like everyone—both inside and outside your company—knows all the old stories about how and why your company is what it is. But they don't know. Sure, I've told our stories so many times that a lot of our team members can recite them. But there are always new team members who are hearing them for the first time. They need to hear those stories because they're a part of who we are. If your team doesn't know about the roots from which your business grew, it's way too easy to wander from your mission or become too comfortable, no matter how good your intentions are.

I get that you might not be the cheerleader type. You don't have to paint your face blue or ride a horse and carry a big sword like William Wallace in the movie *Braveheart* (though that would be awesome). But your team needs to feel your intensity. That's how you empower them to carry your business forward even faster. And yes, you're going to have to repeat yourself on a regular basis. Saying something once is a nice way to hear yourself talk. Saying it a million times is a great way to get your team to hear it, remember it, and live it out.

REFLECT AND RESPOND

In my book *EntreLeadership*, I talk about why micromanagement, when it's the result of a leader's lack of confidence and emotional maturity, often has negative consequences for their ability to grow their business. As a leader, you *do* want to avoid micromanaging your team, but the problem I see more often is a leader getting so wrapped up *not* being a micromanager that they end up avoiding or ignoring responsibilities that *are* part of good leadership. I hit on this briefly when talking about delegation for the Treadmill Operator. One example of that is training a new team member. It's not micromanagement to first walk through every step and then check in on every detail as a new team member learns their role. Once they've proven their integrity and competency, you can begin to more fully delegate that responsibility. In this case, you're serving your team member by setting them up to win.

It's also not micromanagement to check on things you have fully delegated. Every time we do an event, I walk around the venue to get the lay of the land. I meet with the AV guys, and we talk about the opening video of the event. I check out the seats farthest from the stage. I evaluate everything.

My inspection does a few things. First, it gives me confidence that we're ready for the event. Our Live Events Team is a group of thoroughbreds that consistently pulls off events that exceed audience expectations. But in my role, I can never surrender 100 percent of the oversight. That's lazy leadership and will allow the company to stray from its vision.

Second, my team learns what I value and what's important to me based on the things I pay attention to most. People who've been on the team for a while and have worked on a few events with me have learned what I'm going to ask about, and they have the answers before I even ask the questions. I've trained them to look for the things I look for. That's the whole idea behind the concept of "inspect what you expect."

This same idea applies to your entire business. As I've mentioned, our operating board takes time every year to reflect on how things are going across the entire company. We look at our team's health, our strategy, our operations, and our competition. We make sure we're staying true to our mission, vision, and values while challenging ourselves to shoot any sacred cows that might be holding us back.

Now, when you have the honest answers to those questions and they're not the answers you wanted, you have to do something about it. You must respond or even the most insignificant issues will grow and grow until they blow up in your face. And here is the real key to resolving the issues you uncover: Tell your team. This goes back to your culture of overcommunication. Don't hide what's going on from your team. You'll actually need to overshare to get them—and keep them—energized to attack the problems with you.

That's the reason why I have our CFO get on stage at our staff meeting once a month and walk the team through our profit-sharing report. He breaks down how we did last month, then compares the numbers year over year. And if those numbers are down, he shares the context as to why. Maybe we had a landmark month the prior year that we're competing with—or maybe we missed our goals and need to kick it up a notch to get back on track. We talk about it all so by the time a team member sees the profit sharing in their check, they know what to expect. That may seem like overkill, but the fact is, it's impossible to completely withhold important information from your team. Somehow, they'll sense something is up, and they'll create their own stories, and those stories will be ten times worse than the truth. Don't let the worst-case-scenario thinking get out of control. When in doubt—overshare.

PROACTIVE DISRUPTION

One of the most valuable things you can do as the leader of a Peak Performer business is to challenge the status quo. As you reflect on how your company is doing and respond to the issues you find, you're guaranteed to run into areas or processes that seem to be working just fine. But there's something in you that asks, *Could it work better?* That's what proactive disruption is all about, and it's the ultimate manifestation of your culture of relentless improvement. As a leader, you need to break things before they're broken to keep your business moving forward and keep your team energized. You've got to shock the organizational system so you can stay ahead of problems and fix things before they become bigger issues for the company. Be proactive rather than reactive.

I did this with our operating board a few years back when I asked our leadership team what it would take for us to be a $500 million company. That question shifted the focus from the status quo and put the spotlight on the systems and teams we would need to overhaul for the business to operate at that level. We argued through all the options until the entire board was on the same page. The result was that we got ahead of a bunch of obstacles because we changed how we were doing things before those issues ever became restraints for us.

Today, this kind of disruption is owned by our Special Projects Committee. This group of high-level leaders works on large broken things, incubates new ideas or projects that don't have a home inside a department, and breaks things before they are broken. Essentially, this hyper-entrepreneurial work group is tasked with throwing lightning bolts through the business with the goal of beating back complacency. Their work sends a signal to the whole organization that only excellence will be tolerated and that we're going to cause the wave of change instead of be crushed by it.

Even if you don't have a dedicated committee, you can engage in proactive disruption by simply asking yourself and your leadership team challenging questions like: If we wanted to 10x our business, what should we be doing differently right now? Who would we hire? What equipment would we need? Are our current facilities adequate if we double or triple the size of our business?

Now, it may feel risky to push the envelope like this. You're a Peak Performer with a successful business, after all. Why rock the boat? Let me ask you a question. Do you remember these names?

- Sears
- Blockbuster
- Kodak
- Nokia
- Red Lobster

- Toys "R" Us
- Circuit City
- RadioShack
- Kmart

I bet you (or your parents) have shopped at one of those businesses. At some point, each of them was a Peak Performer business. Leaders in their industries. And then, each of them got complacent. They experienced success, allowed themselves to take a foot off the gas for a hair too long, and lost that relentless drive for excellence. And now, they either no longer exist or are in the final phases of disappearing and are effectively dead.

My business was born out of my desperation to get out of bankruptcy, and many of us in business have a similar story. Desperation's good for the soul—it'll push your butt along. But what happens when you're no longer in survival mode? When you're winning and the desperation of the early days is a distant memory? What will drive you then? Here's what I've learned: Sometimes solutions to problems in your business can bubble up from the bottom. And that's great. That's why you work so hard to build an excellent team. But the relentless drive for excellence does not bubble up from the bottom. It comes from you. It comes from your gut. It doesn't accidentally happen. You've got to create it. You've got to continually pour energy into your business. You can't ever take your foot off the gas.

What Winning Looks Like

As a Peak Performer, it's up to you to defend the company culture and world-class expectations of your team against your true enemy—complacency. The components we covered in this chapter are essential for accomplishing that:

- Recommit to your mission
- Inspire your team
- Reflect and respond
- Proactive disruption

You'll know you're winning as a Peak Performer when you look for signs of complacency but can't find them. Your team will still have their scrappy spirit and drive for excellence. Your renewed commitment to your mission keeps you motivated and engaged so you can cast a compelling vision and challenge processes—even when they seem to be working on the surface. Growth and progress are second nature in your company, due in large part to a vibrant culture based on a shared commitment to the organization's values. Everyone from the top down is rowing in the same direction, and you spend most of your time addressing critical, high-impact initiatives—whether that's new opportunities, major challenges, or broken processes.

Thanks to the financial success your company has already experienced, your business can focus on long-term goals and take full advantage of the culture of innovation and continuous improvement you and your leadership team have built. As you look ahead to the Legacy Builder stage, you'll need to have all these elements in sync to maintain the excellence that will solidify your business as a Peak Performer and ensure that you'll have a legacy worth leaving.

Scan the QR code below to get a comprehensive step-by-step action plan with tools and resources that will help you maintain your dominance in the marketplace!

Client Success Story

Arlan Campbell, Steel Tech Building Systems

Arlan Campbell is the founder and CEO of Steel Tech Building Systems in Monett, Missouri. This business is a fantastic example of a company in the Peak Performer stage of business. Steel Tech Building Systems started in 2008 with no employees and no revenue. In 2024, Steel Tech had almost ninety team members and $35 million in revenue. Wow! They describe themselves as "a privately held company that rejects a mindset that cares only about the bottom line. Our values drive our decision-making."

Before building Steel Tech Building Systems from the ground up in 2008, Arlan was a custom home builder just looking to expand his business. He was using a lot of structural steel in many of the large homes they were building and found himself intrigued by the steel structure business.

With custom homes, Arlan was used to contracting out the various aspects of the build (framing, electrical, plumbing, and so on) without actually working with those skills. But constructing a steel building was different. Arlan got to work in the trenches beside the other guys—building relationships and growing together. As someone who feels called to help mentor and equip young men to do life well, Arlan felt this kind of work was more purposeful. And he was all in.

While this new steel business was getting started, Arlan realized he didn't know much about how to build and run a business, much less how to build a solid team. At the time, he and his wife happened to be taking *Financial Peace University* (FPU), and their class coordinator mentioned the *EntreLeadership* book. Arlan picked up a copy and listened to the audiobook on CD while personally delivering the first steel building they had completed, driving from Missouri to Florida.

On the road, Arlan absorbed the content and thought, *This is exactly what I need.* He's been on a continual path of learning—and implementing what he's learned—ever since. Now, Steel Tech is a great example of a business that's run well and obviously cares for its team.

"I've realized that I really can fulfill my purpose here of mentoring young people, and I can learn how to run a business better," Arlan explained.

But of course, Steel Tech has dealt with complacency at times.

"When we're making things happen, we can have this false sense of security that everything is good," Arlan said. "But the reality is that you can be building this great shell of something on the outside—where everything is not good on the inside. We can get complacent that someone else will take care of all the numbers or all the details. We can get complacent in a lack of diligence in maintaining what we've started."

Steel Tech's website captures the heart of what Arlan wants to fight to maintain: "Our goal is service with excellence. We aim to serve our clients so well that they would never think about going elsewhere. Their trust in us is valued and carefully guarded." Keeping a focus on the care and integrity that were laid as the foundation of the business is part of avoiding the trap of complacency for Steel Tech.

"I want to build a business, team, and culture built on integrity in every area of this company," Arlan shared.

He recalls a job where four of his team members had gone to a client's location to fix a mistake—a mistake that they had allowed to happen on the Steel Tech end. As they worked to correct it, Arlan's team discovered problems with the way the building had been erected by an outside company. Without question, they knew the right thing to do was to correct those problems while they were fixing their own mistakes.

"It frustrates me that we made that kind of mistake," Arlan admitted. "But I'm really thankful for the group of people we have here who are owning that mistake. During our meeting, the guy who made the mistake stood up and took responsibility." That's integrity in action—and a great example of a team living out its values, not just slapping them up on a wall.

Over the years, Arlan has found himself wrestling with many different aspects of the business as he and his leadership team have homed in on their values and what it means to make decisions based on those values. He's had to step in to overhaul a system that had been in place for a while and was developed internally—because it was causing siloed work and problems within the company. He's also had to make the gut-wrenching decision to let a few team members go. Arlan can remember days of pure exhaustion and days when he questioned whether he really had what it takes to do this.

In those moments, God pointed Arlan's thoughts back to his purpose, which has always been to be a blessing and to help young people grow personally and professionally.

"If it's just about the money, there will be times when the money's not there, and you'll just want to quit," Arlan said. "There has to be something more that keeps you going when you don't feel like going."

Like many business owners in the Peak Performer stage, Arlan has discovered that you'll spend a huge amount of effort and life on building a business—so it has to be something worth investing in. And you have to know what it is that keeps you going.

"The Momentum Theorem carries us through those low places when we wonder if we're qualified to do this," Arlan explained. "The momentum that has come from our focused intensity over a long period of time carries us through those dips—and it levels out the highs."

LEGACY BUILDER

KEY CHALLENGE:

You don't have a plan for passing on your business.

WHAT WINNING LOOKS LIKE:

The business is successfully running
without requiring your presence.

LEGACY BUILDER

The first time I looked through the glass from outside our studio and watched someone else take calls on *The Dave Ramsey Show*, the earth shifted under my feet. It shouldn't have been a shock. My leadership team and I had been talking about the company's succession plan for years, and a big part of that plan was to raise up new Ramsey Personalities—people who could join me in reaching new audiences and continue our mission to change lives when I wasn't around anymore. And here was the evidence that our plan was working. Our Ramsey Personalities were handling calls and helping people, giving them the same advice I would. That was great news for the company. But what did it mean for me?

I was still wrestling with that reality when one day, just a couple of years ago now, *The Dave Ramsey Show* disappeared forever with one small—intentional—change. Instead of saying, "Welcome to *The Dave Ramsey Show*," as I had for almost thirty years to begin the show, I said, "Welcome to *The Ramsey Show*." That's all. There was no announcement. No fanfare on social media. Just no more Dave. We wondered if anyone would notice. You know who noticed? I did.

It was really distressing and much more emotional than I was prepared for. I got off the air and didn't know what to think. I had built huge brand equity with *my* name—I was the guy who went bankrupt and had scratched and clawed to fight my way out of it. I'd worked my tail off for decades to build a company to help people with their money. I started all of this. My name is all over the building and everything we do. This is who I am.

My friend John Maxwell says, "Where there is no succession, there is no success." The truth is, Ramsey Solutions and its legacy are not about me. The business belongs to God. I'm just the manager. If I let my emotions get in the way of the succession plan my leadership team and I have laid out, all the blood, sweat, and tears we poured into building it would disappear with me.

As a Legacy Builder, your goal is to work yourself out of a job, and in this chapter, we'll talk about the tactical and strategic steps you'll take as part of this stage of business. If you don't execute a good succession plan, you will kill the thing you love just to protect your ego. But I need to warn you, watching your succession plan work will be more emotional than you think. None of the changes we've made as part of our succession plan have been accidental. They have worked exactly as intended. And yes, I was in on all of the planning. It's both depressing and awesome at the same time. Why? Because I planned to be less important, and damned if it didn't work.

I'm constantly asked if I'm ever going to retire, and my answer is always the same: "I'll retire when I quit making sense on the radio." That's because I still enjoy what I do. So I'll keep doing the radio show and podcasts and conference teaching as long as I can. But the CEO part requires that I step away before I "want" to for my son, Daniel's, sake as president of the company—and for the sake of the business as a whole.

LEAVING A LEGACY

No matter what you've done up to this point in your life and business, you *are* going to leave a legacy. The only question is whether it's going to be a good one. Too many owners wait until the last possible moment to hand off their businesses—and even then, their plan is to simply toss the keys to the next guy as they fall into the grave. You can guess how that turns out: Confusion causes morale to tank throughout the company. Key team members leave in droves, customers and vendors lose confidence, and revenue plummets. Inexperienced new leaders make financial mistakes while hefty estate taxes force the sale of valuable assets. The family squabbles over leadership roles, disrupting operations and dividing the team. The outgoing leader takes vital corporate knowledge with him, leaving the new leader struggling to figure things out on their own. New leadership fails to align with the company's core values, and the original mission becomes a fuzzy memory. Legal battles over ownership drain resources and tarnish the company's reputation.

That's a really bleak picture that one too many businesses will face. In his personal research on leadership,

Dr. J. Robert Clinton found that less than 30 percent of leaders finish well. I want to be a leader who finishes well. You can think I'm being morbid if you want to, but we've done detailed research on this subject, and it turns out, none of us is getting out of this alive. Your feelings about your mortality don't outweigh that fact that you have an expiration date. And if you don't have a succession plan, your business's expiration will occur soon after your own. If you want to leave a legacy you can be proud of, you need to decide on a strategy and a succession plan *long before* you exit your company.

SIGNS YOU MAY BE IN THE
LEGACY BUILDER STAGE

You have leveled up through all the other stages.

You are mentally, emotionally, and financially prepared to step away from the business.

You have a clear plan in place to make a successful succession to the new owners of the business.

FRUSTRATIONS YOU FACE IN THE
LEGACY BUILDER STAGE

You want your business to live long past you but don't
know how to hand it off well.

You know if you don't do something, the business is
going to end when you're done.

You realize you're not ready to hand off the business.

The next generation doesn't seem ready to lead the
business.

You don't have children to pass the business to when
you're done.

You're going to have to sell the business to your kids to
fund your retirement.

To be clear, the Legacy Builder stage is not the stage where
you create your succession plan. That work should happen
long before. This is the stage where you start to implement
your succession plan. Our handoff at Ramsey Solutions
became a topic of serious discussion in 2014, but we actually
began talking about what we were going to do with our succession plan five years before that as a matter of stewardship.

Today, we're 100 percent in the Legacy Builder stage. That said, succession plans are like trees. The best time to plant a tree is twenty years ago. The second-best time to plant a tree is today. In our case, we're handing the business off to family. That handoff is almost already done—I'm just hanging around to spread hate and dissension.

All kidding aside, I'm passionate about my daily work, so I'll continue doing it. However, I've been focusing less on the key details and tactical aspects of the company lately. That doesn't mean I'm not doing anything. And I'm not planning to quit tomorrow. I'm just not doing as much as I used to. Today, I'm much more focused on new things, big things, broken things, and a lot of creative, content-related projects—like this book. I stay plugged in to those things because I enjoy them and I'm good at them, but the business can run without me.

KEYS TO A SOLID HANDOFF

The truth is, you have lots of options for how you'll exit the company. You could hand the company over to a family member in the next generation like we are at Ramsey. And one day, I'll write a book about the challenges and blessings of running a family business. But you could also hand your business to your team, sell it, or take it public. You could even shut the company down. I'm not recommending a certain plan, but your plan does need to be certain. And it will need to cover these three areas we'll dig into throughout the rest of this chapter:

- The legal and financial transfer
- The leadership transfer
- The reputation transfer

THE LEGAL AND FINANCIAL TRANSFER

The legal and financial transfer of your business requires a lot of thought, planning, and time to execute. The wrong choices in this area can cost you a ton of money—especially in estate taxes—and can even put the future of the business at risk. I am a big fan of not paying more taxes than I have to. Some people have qualms about that, but there's nothing morally wrong with doing all you can to legally avoid paying taxes. Too many businesses are ruined because they don't handle taxes properly. Don't let that happen to your legacy. Different ownership structures like trusts, family limited partnerships, or limited liability companies have different tax advantages. Other strategies like a phased ownership transfer and using your annual gift tax exclusions and/or the unified estate tax credit can help gradually transfer business ownership and spread out that tax burden over several years.

Do yourself a favor and gather a team of professionals you can lean on to plan a transfer of ownership that will benefit your business. That begins with outside legal counsel with extensive experience in estate planning and business law. You want someone who has a track record of handling complex transfers, knows current tax law backward and forward, and takes a strategic approach to help your business avoid potential legal and financial pitfalls. You should feel like you're their only client because their advice is specific to your family and your business and they're constantly looking out for you by keeping up with changes in the law that might affect your plans.

At Ramsey, we decided on the unusual route of handing the business over to family rather than selling it to them, and we've reached the point in our plan where ownership of Ramsey Solutions has transferred to the Ramsey Family Trust. This was a strategic decision that will give us long-term tax benefits—the trust won't get taxed generationally.

If we hadn't gone this route, the estate tax could have ruined Ramsey because we don't have hundreds of millions of dollars in cash lying around.

Another interesting option is to transfer ownership to your employees through an Employee Stock Option Plan (ESOP) where your employees become owners of some or all of the business. You can get some tax advantages this way, but what I like about it is that the business stays with the people who are the most invested in its success. Depending on the size of your company, an ESOP transfer can be a long process—it's definitely not something you can knock out in a week or so. That's why you need to start thinking about it now, so you can make sure it's done the right way. I've seen ESOPs go bad, so make sure you know all the risks and work with real pros to put one in place.

Early on, you'll need to determine the value of your business. This can be tricky, so you'll need to get a professional accountant on your team who can help you figure out the true worth of your business by looking at your assets, earnings, and market conditions. If you have a high-value business that's worth more than $20 million, talk with your accountant about using minority interests to devalue certain aspects of your business. For example, in an LLC, a minority interest isn't worth as much pro rata as a majority interest, and recognizing this can lower the overall valuation, providing a realistic and fair assessment of your business's worth. That will make the transfer more manageable and tax efficient and set a solid foundation for the next phase of the business. This kind of stuff is fun for me, so it may seem like I'm getting into the weeds here. The good thing is, you don't have to know all the rules and regulations if you work with a professional to help you navigate it all.

When it comes to the actual sale or transfer of the business, the terms of the deal are key, beginning with a sale price that matches the financial health of the business and the future plans of the new owners. Generally, the sale price would not exceed five times the net profit of the business. If you aim for four times the net profit, you'll not only make the business more attractive to potential buyers, but you'll also ensure a sustainable financial future for the business itself. Overpricing just makes it harder for the new owners to manage and grow the business—which is not great if you want to have a lasting legacy. I've seen financial transfers have a lot of success when both parties agree on a lower initial sale price with owner financing terms that the seller will receive a large percentage of the profits as payment until the agreed sale price is met. This kind of percentage-of-profit-financing agreement means the buyer isn't facing a huge financial strain if the business doesn't generate immediate high profits, and the seller (you) has the security of knowing you'll get the agreed amount. Win-win.

Yes, there's a lot of pressure to get your business's legal and financial transfer just right, but the process doesn't have to be overwhelming if you approach it methodically. Start by putting together your team of professionals. I can't stress enough how important that is. Then, by taking strategic steps, you can plot out an ownership transfer that will secure your legacy of years of hard work and dedication while setting up the business and its new owners for future success. That's how you transfer ownership of a business that will outlive you.

THE LEADERSHIP TRANSFER

Your leadership transfer has two important components: your leadership team and, even more critical, your successor. Ever since you were a Trailblazer, you've been building and pouring into your leadership team. Now, in the Legacy Builder stage, your leadership team has to be at a level where they can run the company in your absence. They know the decisions you would make and why you would make them. They guide the team based on the company's core values and take as much ownership of the mission and vision as you do. They represent all areas of the business, bring different strengths and perspectives, and have established radical levels of honesty and trust over time. If you think that's impossible, let me tell you, Ramsey Solutions has had a leadership team like this for many years now, and it's been a tremendous blessing. Most importantly for this stage of our business, the people on my leadership team are full partners with me in our company's succession plan.

In the same way it takes time to build a leadership team that can continue your legacy, the person you choose as your successor needs time to grow and step into that role. You need time to train them to be the right kind of owner. They need time to build a reputation in the business and be recognized for their capabilities in everyday interactions. Your goal is for them to be the obvious choice in the eyes of the team long before formal decisions are made in the boardroom.

This is particularly true for family-owned businesses. My son, Daniel, became president of Ramsey Solutions early in

2023. While he's been in other leadership roles for a long time now, he was never guaranteed the president's role. In fact, when Daniel first joined the team over ten years ago, we didn't even talk about him one day leading Ramsey Solutions. The pressure of that expectation was too much for a young guy in his early twenties just starting his career. He just wanted to be part of the team and learn to be a good salesperson. As time went on and Daniel continued to excel in every role we put him in, we moved him into a vice president leadership position and began to turn up the heat on the conversations about his long-term role with the company.

Those conversations, of course, included our leadership team who were the first to know about the plan to eventually move Daniel into the presidency. We talked to our team about it, too, so they all had an understanding of the changes that were coming and the goal behind them. We also shared the relevant parts of our succession plan with our vendors. The Legacy Builder has to commit to an open, ongoing dialogue about the future of the business. Otherwise, people will fill in the gaps with doubt and rumors, and neither are helpful for the legacy you want to leave.

Another part of our plan to set Daniel up for success in his role was long-term mentoring. I had three of my operating board members meet with Daniel every Friday morning. I excluded myself from that mentoring group on purpose. I wanted these three top leaders to pour their knowledge, experience, and insight into Daniel and help him prepare for the responsibilities he'd take on as president. Once he officially became president, Daniel and I started having one-on-one meetings every Thursday morning to focus on the business and accountability. As his leader, I'm looking for any way that I can assist him and push things forward as needed. We've had a blast as father and son working together as the CEO and president, and we aren't done yet. In the future, I will begin to peel away from my current leadership responsibilities while Daniel takes on more and more of the company leadership. Eventually, I'll be just another Personality, hosting the show, speaking at events, and writing books, and I'll keep doing that as long as I can.

One more note about passing your business on to a family member—and it's a tough one: You'll need to make it clear to both family and non-family leadership that the succession plan is contingent on your successor's future conduct and your relationship with them. It is not a guarantee. In other words, if they fail to live up to the expectations you set for them in terms of conduct, personal growth, and commitment to the mission, you have the right to remove them from the succession plan.

Gradual succession plans are the most successful succession plans. That becomes really clear in the leadership transfer because it takes time to build your leadership team, identify the person you'll trust to take the lead in your place, and then empower them to actually do that. It also takes time for your team and other businesses you work with to understand and get comfortable with the changes that are coming, and you'll have to keep those lines of communication open for as long as it takes to see your plan through.

THE REPUTATION TRANSFER

Rush Limbaugh was known as the voice of American conservatism and had the number one talk show on radio in America. He was number one, Sean Hannity was number two, and we were number three. I was blessed to spend time with Rush on several different occasions, and whether you liked him or not, there was no denying Rush was an icon— a bigger-than-life personality. He single-handedly brought AM radio back to life and pretty much invented the radio talk show genre. Not only did he become the industry standard, but he also had unbelievable influence and power with the top levels of our country's political leadership. But he had absolutely zero succession plan when he died at age seventy in 2021. His brand recognition and influence were completely lost much too quickly when he died.

His story, and way too many like it, was a warning sign to me. I decided we were going to approach the awkward succession planning process and fight through it so we wouldn't lose everything we've built. Ramsey Solutions is on a mission to change the toxic culture, and we can't afford to lose ground by making the mistake of having *no plan*. So a huge part of our succession plan is making sure the brand—our reputation in the marketplace—can stand without me.

Now, I'll admit, there's a good chance this part of your succession plan will look different from ours. It all depends on how much of the brand is built solely on you personally. Back in 2012, we created this weird metric we called "non-Dave revenue" so we could track how much the business made on products and initiatives that didn't involve me. It was only 7 percent when we first measured it, meaning if something were to happen to me, 93 percent of the business revenue would essentially disappear.

To fix this, we came up with what we now call our Survivability Index that measures the percentage of the business that will survive when I am no longer a part of it. Then we began making strategic moves to increase that rating. One of those moves was changing the name of *The Dave Ramsey Show* to *The Ramsey Show*. We'd been working toward the change for a while, and by the time we pulled the trigger, our Personalities were old pros at co-hosting the show—with me and without me. They were handling calls just like I would, and the change was having little to no impact on our ratings. We didn't make a formal announcement about the name change because we wanted to minimize any disruption with our six hundred-plus affiliates. But several attentive YouTube viewers spotted the change, and that was enough to spark rumors that I was about to leave the show.

Our next move was to change the name of our website from daveramsey.com to ramseysolutions.com. It wasn't just a marketing move. Removing my name from our web address was a major step in ensuring the future of the company. However, it did have short-term consequences. Our website traffic took a big hit, and it took longer than we liked to regain trust and credibility with the search engines.

The good thing about these steps at this stage is that we call the shots on the timing, and instead of weathering these storms all at once after something happens to me, we could deal with them one at a time—while I was still around, being very active within the company. And it's a strategy that's paying off. Our Survivability Index has soared into the ninetieth percentile, which means Ramsey Solutions is much less dependent on me and is in a much better position for long-term success.

Your business's brand may not be as dependent on you as founder and owner, but your business does have a reputation to transfer from you to your successor. In the same way we took small steps with our audience to build trust with our Personalities over time, your customers, vendors, and team need to see you working with and training up your successor and see your overall succession plan. Then, when you step away, there will be a healthy level of trust that things will continue to work after you're gone. Otherwise, your customers, vendors, and team will have no choice but to assume that when the old guy dies, the whole business will fall apart. As with all the other aspects of this stage, time is your friend. The more time you have to pour into your plan and the more time your customers, vendors, and team have to adjust to your business's new leadership, the better your chances of a successful reputation handoff.

WHAT WINNING LOOKS LIKE

When you get to the Legacy Builder stage, you've put in the work it takes for your business to thrive. That by itself is a huge achievement! Now your focus is on how your business will continue to thrive after you're gone, and a solid succession plan is the key to making that happen. Here are the succession plan elements we covered:

- The legal and financial transfer
- The leadership transfer
- The reputation transfer

Right now, the financial and legal transfer might feel like the biggest and most complex part of your succession plan. And you're not wrong. As I said, mistakes in this area could limit your business's future, if not destroy it. But once you have your team of experts to help you with the accounting and legal issues, you should feel some of that weight come off your shoulders. At that point, your biggest concern is checking progress and making sure your successor and leadership team are fully invested in making the plan work.

What will likely come as a shock—and it was for me too—is the roller coaster of emotions you'll deal with as you walk through your succession plan. You can be as business minded as you want to about it. You can discuss every aspect of your plan a million times from a hundred different angles and with as many people as you want. You can develop your plan over decades if you want to, but when you finally pull the trigger and start to see your plan fall into place, your ego will take a hit. You're going to have that moment when you wonder what it means for you and your identity now that your business no longer needs you the way it used to. And the irony is that this disturbing realization is the best indicator you have that your succession plan is working—that you're winning as a Legacy Builder!

Maybe that's really why so many business owners don't create a succession plan. They're afraid to figure out who they are separate from the business they've put so much of themselves into over the years. For this reason, it's very difficult to hand off a business that's all about you. We have found the succession plan has a much higher probability of working when the owner has a higher calling than simply being in charge. When the current generation views the business as something bigger than themselves, they will nobly rise above their own emotions and self-interest for the good of the business and possibly their family. As people of faith, we view Ramsey Solutions as owned by God, and I am just the manager.

Good managers plan for their handoff where a selfish owner might not. Business is noble, and if you believe in what you're doing, you will want it to live on after you leave. The Legacy Builder stage of business is not about you or your ego. It's about managing your business for God and setting it up to be successful and sustainable after you're done.

Scan the QR code below to get a comprehensive step-by-step action plan with tools and resources that will help you set your business up to continue its impact long after you leave the business.

CONCLUSION

It was truly a historic moment and an amazing accomplishment. On November 15, 1805, Meriwether Lewis and William Clark stood at the mouth of the Columbia River and looked out at the vastness of the Pacific Ocean in front of them. Exactly one year, six months, and one day earlier, they'd set out from St. Louis, Missouri, in search of the legendary Northwest Passage to the sea. They were the first ever to map this journey, and eventually, nearly half a million settlers would make that same trip. But instead of eighteen months, it would take them less than five months—over 300 percent faster! How could they do it so quickly? Because someone had gone before them and marked the way.

As a business owner, you no doubt feel like you're exploring uncharted territory—and you often are. But it doesn't have to feel that way, and you don't have to feel as though you're completely alone in a business wilderness. Learn from those who have gone before you and mapped the way. My hope is that this book will do for you what Lewis and Clark did for all the settlers who came after them—provide direction and hope.

What you've read in this book won't give you a magic wand you can wave to make running your business easy. It will still take your blood, sweat, and tears to win at business. But I hope that this book will guide you to save time, money, and wasted effort. By sharing Ramsey Solutions' ups and downs—our mistakes, wrong turns, and eventual solutions—I believe we can help you build a business you love and leave a legacy you're proud of.

If you've read this far, you've learned about our system and how to win at business. You've learned principles that will grow your business and your team. You now have important knowledge to guide your choices. But you could use one more thing—consider it pure jet fuel for your journey through the Five Stages of Business.

We've developed a digital platform where you'll find a set of tools that automate many of the processes we talked about as we unpacked the stages. This digital platform is called EntreLeadership Elite. The tools in Elite are designed to align your team and simplify the process of accountability for leaders and team members. You'll be able to gauge team unity while driving and tracking progress toward your goals. Trying to do that manually would be practically impossible when your business grows at the speed the EntreLeadership System will cause. We know these tools work because we created them for ourselves first—they've all been tested, tweaked, improved, and used every week with our team. And EntreLeadership Elite makes it possible for you to share these tools with your team, taking out the guess work and grunt work of working the EntreLeadership System. You can get started using Elite here:

Drivers and Stages Recap

Let me remind you of the Six Drivers of Business. They drive your business forward and are essential for its success.

Personal: You're both the problem and the solution.
Purpose: Business is about more than just the bottom line.

People: A unified team is key to winning.

Plan: Success is intentional; it doesn't happen by accident.

Product: Serve enough people and the revenue will follow.

Profit: Profits fuel your purpose.

Remember, as you master these six drivers, they will propel you through the Five Stages of Business:

Treadmill Operator: You're making too much of the money yourself.

Pathfinder: You struggle to get your team pointed in the right direction.

Trailblazer: You need a leadership team and strategic plan.

Peak Performer: You must defend the culture you created.

Legacy Builder: Your business thrives after you're gone.

This is the EntreLeadership System, and it's the method we've used to go from my starting this business on a card table in my living room to having a $250-million-a-year business. We still have a lot of work to do. But we're winning at it. And I want you to win at business too. You'll create wealth for yourself and your family. But even more than that, you'll shape culture and influence the world. Bob Briner talks about this in his book *Roaring Lambs*. He explains that you're not called to sit on the sidelines or retreat from the mainstream. You are to boldly live out your values and your faith, right where God has placed you—in the middle of your business.

See, there are primarily two kinds of people running businesses today. First, you'll find those who are self-centered. These are the typical greedy jerks who are all about money, shortcuts, and taking advantage of others. Their primary goal is to serve themselves.

The second kind of people running businesses are those who are others-centered—selfless. I believe that's where you are if you're reading this book. Your primary goal is to serve others through your work. You want to help your clients, your team, and the economy. Your team members have jobs because of you. You're a contributor to your community because your goods and services make people's lives better. That's being others-centered, and it makes a positive impact in the world. You're not being selfish; you're being a servant.

The marketplace needs more of those kinds of business owners because the more of us there are, the less room there is for the selfish ones. Here's what I mean: I know a musician who is crazy about Jesus and loves making music. Even though he's a strong Christian, most of his songs are what most people would call "secular" hits, meaning they don't talk explicitly about his faith. However, this is a man of God serving with integrity in a business that's often filled with self-serving people who don't care what kind of filth they produce as long as it creates profit for them. When he has a hit song on the radio, even if he doesn't mention the name of Jesus, he is displacing other trashy songs that could have been taking up that airtime. At the same time, he is serving as an example, showing others in the industry that you can be successful in the music business without giving in to toxic cultural norms.

The same thing happens when a Christian teacher steps into a classroom or when a Christian politician runs for office or when a Christian businessman opens a business. All they need to do is serve with excellence, keep their integrity, and maintain their commitment to God to make a huge impact for the Kingdom. Just by *being there*, they are displacing the forces of the enemy.

I look around this country and see honest, brave, and noble leaders. They're true servant leaders. Leaders like you. Your business isn't just a way to make money—it's a platform to make an impact. The way you treat your team, clients, and vendors can create positive change that goes well beyond profits and will leave a legacy you may not see this side of heaven.

Business is hard, but your business is also important to the world we live in. Don't play it safe. Use your business as a force for good. Just like Briner's roaring lambs, let your business be a powerful voice that shows the world that success and faith *can* go hand in hand. When you do that, you're not only taking your business to the next level—you're playing a part in transforming the world for the better.

FINAL THOUGHTS

Winston Churchill was a little guy—about five foot six. A bulldog of a man and quite a character to say the least. And if it weren't for him, we'd likely all be speaking German right now. He came to power as British prime minister during World War II in a weird way. In September of 1938, Adolf Hitler invaded Poland. By 1940, Hitler was going through Europe like a hot knife through butter. Neville Chamberlain, then prime minister, however, was one of those fools who thought you could negotiate with evil—the kind of evil represented by Hitler. His strategy was not to show strength but to appease. But there's no appeasing a madman. Obviously, his strategy didn't work.

Wisely, the English people rose up. In May of 1940, Parliament unseated Chamberlain and made Churchill the Prime Minister. Churchill took the opportunity to lambaste Chamberlain, saying, "You were given the choice between war and dishonor. You chose dishonor, and now you will have war." His message to Hitler was equally clear: "We will never negotiate." And it became a rallying cry for the entire United Kingdom as Hitler relentlessly bombed London night after night for eighteen long months.

During the bombing raids, Churchill, widely considered one of the greatest orators in history, would give fabulous speeches to encourage the British people. Churchill even gave speeches before the United States Congress in an attempt to find another ally in their war effort. He would have to wait until the Japanese bombed Pearl Harbor in December of 1941 to get the help he needed. Until then, this little guy with a huge voice held the entire United Kingdom together.

Early in 1941, before America changed everything by entering the war, Harrow School, the school Churchill attended as a boy, asked him to speak at a graduation ceremony later in the year. There are two versions of what happened at this commencement. But the hard-core Churchill supporters mostly agree on this one.

On October 29, 1941, with the war still raging, Churchill walked to the podium, put down his cane, and took off his top hat. He launched into his prepared commencement address, and in the middle of his speech, Churchill said this:

"This is the lesson: Never give in, never give in. Never, never, never, never—in nothing great or small, large or petty—never give in except to convictions of honor and good sense. Never yield to force; never yield to the apparently overwhelming might of the enemy . . . These are not dark days; these are great days—the greatest days our country has ever lived; and we must all thank God that we have been allowed, each of us according to our station, to play a part in making these days memorable in the history of our race."

Then he picked up his hat and cane and walked off the stage. The point of his speech, in the midst of the worst war the world had seen to date, was to never, ever quit. Never quit.

That's so encouraging and inspiring to me. I know you might be running a business that you started simply to make money. Maybe you've had the worst year of your life and you're trying to decide whether you're going to stay open or not. Or maybe you've just been doing your business for fun, but now it's not fun and you want to move on. That's okay. Find something else to do. But even if you've had the worst year of your life, your business is part of who you are. Not in an unhealthy way, but it's knitted on your soul. That's who I am.

If you have the desire to run your business well but feel like quitting, I understand. I've been there more times than I care to remember. I declared bankruptcy on September 23, 1988, and had to start completely over. I've been building and leading Ramsey Solutions for over three decades now. There have been plenty of times when I've thought, *I've had it. I'm tired of all this crap. I'm done.*

But there's something inside me that won't let me just roll over. And there's something inside of you too. So my final words to you are very simple. They're the same thing Churchill told his people:

Don't you dare quit! Never quit, never quit, never quit!

EntreLeadership® ELITE

Your team is the key to winning in every stage of business.

EntreLeadership Elite is the online platform that equips you with tools and training to build a winning team.

Join thousands of business owners already using Elite to **grow themselves, lead their teams, and scale their businesses.**

CLAIM YOUR EXCLUSIVE OFFER FOR ELITE